# TEXAS MASS GRAVES

## BURIAL GROUNDS OF ATROCITY, MASSACRE AND BATTLE

T0274733

KATHY BENJAMIN

THE
History
PRESS

Published by The History Press
Charleston, SC
www.historypress.com

*Front cover, top left*: author's collection; *top center*: author's collection; *top right*: author's collection.
*Back cover, top left*: Goliad County Historical Commission; *top right*: Jim Evans/ Wikimedia Commons (Creative Commons Attribution-Share Alike 4.0 International license).

First published 2022

Manufactured in the United States

ISBN 9781467152488

Library of Congress Control Number: 2022939463

*For my father*

# CONTENTS

# INTRODUCTION

I n 2011, the small town of Hull, Texas, made headlines around the world. The BBC News website blared: "Police to Search Texas Property for Possible Mass Grave."[1] A CBS News headline added more horrible detail: "Police Investigate Reports of Mass Grave with 'a lot of bodies' near Hardin, Texas."[2] The *New York Times* also covered the story. It waited a few hours and so was able to give an accurate report: "In Texas, Mass Grave Report Leads to Drama but No Bodies."[3]

There was no mass grave; there was no grave at all. The stories and police investigation were based solely on a tip called in by a psychic claiming there was a mass grave of dismembered bodies—including children—at the home of a local family.[4]

There is something haunting about the term "mass grave." It is no wonder that even some of the most preeminent news organizations published stories based on very little information. Putting "mass grave" in a headline will drive clicks. The *New York Times*, possibly feeling a bit smug that it was not taken in by the claim, reported the scene outside the house of a perfectly innocent family: "throngs of reporters camped outside the home, two news helicopters circled above, and cable news stations flashed alerts that up to thirty bodies had been found."[5]

Disposing of a body because it is unpleasant and poses a health risk is markedly different from burying a loved one with grave goods or holding a ceremony over the grave. *Homo sapiens* have been ritualistically burying their dead for at least one hundred thousand years. As most rituals don't result in proof in the form of artifacts one hundred millennia later, it's possible that funerals in their most basic form began even earlier. Indeed, ritualistic burial can be considered one of the key developments, along with language and religion, marking our prehistoric ancestors' evolution from animals to humans.

Archaeologists have unearthed examples of mass burials by indigenous civilizations prior to European colonization, although not on a wide scale. Examples in Texas include a mass grave of women and children from the late prehistoric period at the Harrell site in Young County and a Plains Village grave of five individuals at the Dillard site in Cooke County. However, this survey will limit itself to the use and creation of mass graves postcolonization.

While not all civilizations chose to practice rituals that modern Texans would recognize as standard funeral rites, as Timothy W. Wolfe and Clifton D. Bryant write in the *Handbook of Death and Dying, Vol. 1*, there are two aspects of burial (if burial is someone's chosen disposition of their remains) that are vital in our country: "In the United States, we have come to expect that most persons, especially 'respectable' persons, will be buried in their own individual graves with their own markers."[6] This means that the very existence of a mass grave is a sign that at that moment, in some way, society had broken down. The unspoken contract with others—that when we die and are unable to fight for our wishes or rights or even basic human decency, the living will dispose of our remains in a way that is respectful—was not fulfilled. This might be out of disdain or necessity, but the presence of a mass grave almost guarantees that something has gone drastically wrong.

Because of the tragic and often hurried nature of mass graves, oral history and legend can lead to incorrect assumptions, even when not a single psychic is involved. The citizens of Matagorda, Texas, discovered this in 2001.

Sometime in the early twentieth century, local stories centered on an unmarked mound in Matagorda Cemetery resulted in the belief that it contained a mass grave. Ideas as to who was buried there and what killed them varied depending on which version someone heard, but the most common theories were that it was the final resting place of those killed in an 1826 massacre of white settlers by members of the Karankawa tribe, victims of an 1862 yellow fever epidemic or Confederate soldiers who drowned when their boat capsized in 1863. But one thing that all of the stories shared was that this mound was a group burial of individuals who had died in the same tragedy. Locals took great interest in the site, continually adding markers, curbs and other improvements, as well as maintaining the turf.

In 2001, the people of Matagorda invited researchers from the Center of Ecological Archaeology at Texas A&M University to excavate the mass grave so that the truth behind it could finally be revealed. After a century of stories that seemed to put the matter beyond doubt, it must have been shocking to learn that the mound was not, in fact, a mass grave. It was simply a section of the cemetery containing regular, individual burials of six people. They had not died due to a shared, disastrous experience but at different times from about 1850 to 1875. After it learned the truth, the Matagorda Cemetery Association erected a marker at the site detailing the original myth and the real details of the still-nameless individuals buried there.

While the stories of the Matagorda mound may have been inaccurate, at other times, oral history and legend are all the information available about mass graves.

Ambrose Bierce, pictured in 1892, was an author and Civil War veteran. After traveling south to observe the Mexican Revolution, he disappeared without a trace in 1914. Various theories posit that he died by suicide, was executed by a Mexican firing squad or ended up in a mass grave in Marfa, Texas. *Bancroft Library, UC Berkeley.*

This is especially true when it comes to the locations of the burial grounds of people of color, most notably enslaved Black individuals who died before the end of the Civil War.

Even without these complications, it would be impossible to contain the stories of all of the mass graves in Texas in one slim volume. Nor is there one official definition of what constitutes a mass grave, leaving plenty of burials up for interpretation. All of the group burials included here were the last resting places of at least three and usually four or more individuals. In almost all cases, they were buried at the same time, rather than, for example, a single grave for a family that was reopened as each member passed away. And they are all notable, although the reasons why vary greatly.

While modern Texans may think of mass graves as things of the past, each time one of these communal burial sites is uncovered, it brings some of the most painful moments in the state's history into the present. Understanding the events that led to Texas's mass graves allows us to process these tragic events and consider what honoring the dead really means.

# I

# DISEASES AND NATURAL DISASTERS

Mass graves result from clashes with a formidable foe, none more so than Mother Nature. Many of the mass graves in Texas exist not because of intersocietal conflicts but as a result of epidemics, pandemics, tornadoes and hurricanes.

# 1

## YELLOW FEVER

**M**odern-day Texans do not tremble at the mention of "Yellow Jack." In the 1800s, however, this scourge decimated town after town during waves of epidemics. There was no cure and a significant death rate of anywhere from 10 to 60 percent. The Texas Department of State Health Services says that at least thirty thousand people a year still die from the disease around the world.[7] Thankfully, there has not been an outbreak in Texas since 1905, and the past eighty years have seen very few cases in the United States as a whole. While it's now known that mosquitoes transmit yellow fever, in the nineteenth century, all that Texans knew was that the disease struck in the summer but never the winter and seemed to come out of nowhere.

The name "yellow fever" came from the color a victim's skin turned, a result of liver failure and jaundice. At best, a mild case might mean a week of flu-like symptoms. The worst cases saw victims experience incredibly high fevers and vomit black blood before kidney failure, followed by death.

As no one knew for sure how it was transmitted, and as the fear of outbreaks rose to the level of communal panic, newspapers regularly reported on rumors that a case of yellow fever had been diagnosed in any part of the United States, no matter how remote. On October 25, 1873, Austin's *Daily Democratic Statesman* published dispatches from across the country listing the number of deaths from the disease in the previous twenty-four hours in locations as varied as Columbus, Texas—less than one hundred miles from the state capital—and Brooklyn, New York, in two separate columns on the front page.[8]

While cases of yellow fever emerged in Texas every summer, a few years in the second half of the 1800s saw epidemics in the state kill on such a scale that the survivors were forced to resort to mass graves to bury their loved ones, friends and neighbors.

## HOUSTON, 1839 AND 1867

While Houston was originally selected as the capital of the Republic of Texas, an outbreak of yellow fever in 1839 was bad enough for the government to rethink its decision. This was prescient, as Houston would see regular outbreaks over the next few decades.

The first thirty-one burials in Glendale Cemetery are said to have been yellow fever victims placed in a mass grave from that very 1839 epidemic that resulted in "a fearful number of new graves" in the young city of Houston and surrounding area, many of them mass burials.[9] Some cemeteries dug trenches and disposed of bodies without funeral rituals. There were just too many dead for that. Up to 12 percent of the population was killed by yellow fever that year, 240 lives out of about 2,000 residents.

There would be nine more large outbreaks over the next twenty-eight years, but none as bad as 1839. Then came 1867. The disease was probably brought to Houston by General Charles Griffin and his men when they moved their headquarters from Galveston during a yellow fever outbreak on the island. By the time winter put an end to it, almost five hundred Houstonians were dead.

The Harris County Historical Commission marker erected in 2017 by the Memorial Villages Heritage Trail in St. Peter Cemetery—currently in Houston but in an outlying area in the 1800s—highlights the obvious issue that towns faced when so many people died: there was not enough left to bury them. "In 1859 and 1867, yellow fever epidemic killed many church members, among them newly-arrived pastor Rev. M. Hailfinger, in 1859. As many as thirty-six dead were placed in mass graves that are unmarked. 1867, when yellow fever swept through nearby Houston, terrified citizens fled to outlying areas, bringing the disease with them. Dozens of Houstonians and the Spring Branch villagers who cared for them died, and the small community struggled to find enough healthy people for burial crews."[10]

Scientists and historians still have no explanation why, but fortunately for the people of Houston, 1867 saw the last major yellow fever outbreak in that city.

The 1867 yellow fever outbreak in Galveston saw residents racing to get off the island, as seen in this etching showing a wharf with "the panic-stricken citizens fleeing from the yellow fever." *GRANGER.*

CENTRAL WHARF, GALVESTON, TEXAS—THE PANIC-STRICKEN CITIZENS FLEEING FROM THE YELLOW FEVER.

## SABINE PASS, 1862

Ships carrying cargo from farther south were a constant source of yellow fever, made worse during the Civil War thanks to blockade runners. Such a ship is likely what brought the disease to Sabine Pass. Before it subsided, the yellow fever outbreak had killed somewhere between one hundred and two hundred people.

With most of the town's residents having fled at the first sign of danger, few were left to deal with the dead. About thirty Confederate soldiers who were spared the disease buried many of the bodies in mass graves at Sabine Pass Cemetery. Today, these graves are still unmarked. A large, empty field in the middle of the cemetery, where the ground dips slightly, is the only sign of where the yellow fever victims were laid to rest.

## LA GRANGE, 1867

On August 27, 1867, a Mr. C. Sayers died of yellow fever in La Grange. The town had a population of about one thousand. Within two months, over two hundred of them would be dead.

The *New Orleans Crescent*'s headline on September 26, 1867, left no doubt how bad the situation was: "The Yellow Fever in the South—Great Suffering at La Grange, Texas." In a time before instantaneous communication, the paper's information came from someone in the middle of the disaster.

General Charles Griffin survived many of the bloodiest battles of the Civil War only to succumb to yellow fever during the 1867 Galveston epidemic. He died on the island on September 15 of that year, aged forty-one. *Library of Congress Prints and Photographs Division.*

*We have been shown private letters of a perfectly reliable character from La Grange, Texas, which tells a pitiable story of the unparalleled sufferings of the people in that town and its vicinity.*

*Those remaining of the citizens number barely 500 yet the interments have reached as high as 24 in two days. The average mortality is eight. Those stricken by the yellow fever are almost sure to die, the disease proving fatal in nine cases out of ten. Every house in the town is filled with sickness and with death. Business has ceased entirely; the newspapers are no longer published; the jail has been emptied of its inmates, who fled in terror from the scene of desolation. In some cases there is no one to bury the dead. Whole families have been swept away.*[11]

Two weeks later, on October 9, the same paper ran a letter in full, this time from a local man in La Grange, Livingston Lindsay, who was reporting on the situation to Governor Elisha Marshall Pease. The numbers he reported are shocking:

*Our mutual friend, Dr. M. Evans, and his daughter, very unexpectedly to me, and to my great surprise, from the report I had heard of their cases, both departed this life last night, and will be buried today....I don't know certainly—but it does appear to me that this favor [sic] has proved more fatal here—than it has ever been anywhere in the South, or even in the West Indies. Just to think of it—one hundred and seventy deaths, in a period of a little over four weeks, in a population, all told, of not more than 1,600.*[12]

Even in the context of a time when any outbreak of yellow fever was a crisis, the devastation it wrought at La Grange in 1867 was extraordinary. There were so many bodies to bury that the town ran out of coffins. Bodies were left in a heap in the cemetery, waiting for someone to bury them. Mass graves were the obvious expedient, with half a dozen or more people laid to rest at a time. The Texas Historical Commission Marker Number 18523, located at the edge of Old La Grange Cemetery, gives some idea of what the town was facing as more and more people died and their bodies literally piled up:

*In some cases, entire families were lost as caregivers fell ill after tending the sick....While yellow fever affected many communities, its toll on La Grange was catastrophic with fatalities estimated at over 200, fifteen to twenty percent of the total population. Evidence of the epidemic may*

Yellow fever didn't discriminate. One victim of the 1867 epidemic was Sam Houston's widow, Margaret Lea, who died on December 3, 1867, in Independence, Texas, after falling ill with the disease. She was forty-eight years old and left eight children between the ages six and twenty-four. *Thomason Special Collections, Sam Houston State University.*

*be seen in the Old La Grange City Cemetery where a large number of gravestones show deaths from August through October 1867. However, the outbreak was so overwhelming that many victims lie unidentified in mass graves in the northeastern corner of the cemetery. These victims remind us of the once-devastating disease and its effect on early citizens.*[13]

# 2

# CHOLERA

Cholera is still a serious issue in the developing world, with an estimated ninety-five thousand people dying of the disease every year as of 2021, per the Centers for Disease Control (CDC). But this danger has been virtually eliminated in Texas. The Texas Department of State Health Services records that between 2015 and 2019, there was not a single case of cholera in the state. This would have shocked those persons living here in the nineteenth century, for whom cholera outbreaks were a reason to take precautions, up to and including fleeing their homes and not returning until the danger passed, however long that might be.[14]

While there are various ways of catching cholera—including documented cases from eating undercooked or raw shellfish from the Gulf of Mexico—the most common method of transmission is from drinking water contaminated by feces. Unfortunately, this wasn't discovered until the 1850s and, even then, wasn't widely known for decades. The prevailing theory at the time was that cholera resulted from inhaling "miasma," or bad air. In 1849, the year of a major epidemic in Texas, an article in the *Texian Advocate* laid out anecdotal evidence from which it concluded that "cholera is transmitted by atmospheric air alone."[15] This misunderstanding meant recurring worldwide outbreaks throughout the century, starting with the first cholera pandemic to spread beyond Asia, in 1817.

While most people recover from cholera infections and experience little more than mild symptoms, others face extreme diarrhea and vomiting, which can lead to rapid dehydration. In the worst cases, death occurs mere hours after the patient presents symptoms. During nineteenth-century cholera epidemics in Texas, these sudden and numerous deaths could easily overwhelm a town's ability to deal with the bodies.

Major cholera outbreaks in the mid-1830s left whole towns empty. After the 1833 epidemic, town councils in the Mexican settlements north of the Rio Grande were ordered by the governor to add half a vara (about sixteen and a half inches) of dirt over all cemeteries with cholera victims, as there had been so many dead to bury that many graves had not been dug deep enough. When it became clear that cholera had returned in 1834, Goliad moved its cemetery to a different location to avoid "contamination" of the airflow into the town.[16]

## SAN ANTONIO, 1849

The French missionary Abbe Emmanuel Henri Domenech was in Texas and visited San Antonio during the town's 1849 cholera outbreak, which he later wrote about in his book *Missionary Adventures in Texas and Mexico: A Personal Narrative of Six Years' Sojourn in Those Regions.* He describes a city transformed by death: "San Antonio, which a few days before was so gay, so crowded with people, and so full of life, was now silent as the grave. The streets were deserted, and the church bells no longer tolled the ordinary. Had they done so, the tolling would have been continuous night and day. The parish priest could find no time even to say mass."[17]

The abbe estimated that one third of the city was near death. Although this was most certainly an overestimate, it illustrates just how widespread the suffering appeared at the time.[18] In the six weeks the cholera epidemic raged, traditional burial became impossible. Domenech recorded: "We met no one in the streets, save those who were carrying off the dead. Coffins were scarce, and the dead were in many instances strapped to dried ox-hides, and thus dragged along, all livid and purple, to their graves."

## PORT LAVACA, 1849

They were often joined in those graves by others. In Port Lavaca, group burials of victims of the dreaded scourge were some of the first to take place in the town's original cemetery. In 1986, the Texas Historical Commission

The 1849 cholera outbreak that necessitated the mass grave in Port Lavaca Cemetery was not limited to Texas. Former U.S. president James K. Polk died on June 15 in Nashville, Tennessee, a victim of the same epidemic. *Library of Congress.*

erected Marker Number 4077 at the burial ground. The plaque notes that "Burials in this historic cemetery began in the 1840s, with several mass graves dating from an 1849 cholera epidemic."[19]

## VICTORIA, 1846

During the 1846 cholera outbreak in Victoria, "victims died so rapidly that they could not be buried properly, and were hurriedly dumped into shallow excavations in a common burying ground, the present Memorial Square," according to information compiled by the Federal Writers' Project in its Depression-era history *Texas: A Guide to the Lone Star State.*[20] The State Historical Survey Committee erected Marker Number 3327 in the square in 1968. The plaque records that the cemetery at the location was rarely used "until 1846, when a new city ordinance discouraged burials in family cemeteries possibly to combat a cholera epidemic."[21] A shortage of coffins meant victims were often wrapped only in sheets or blankets, wearing the clothes they died in. Again, it seems that the desire to get an overwhelming number of bodies into the ground as quickly as possible resulted in shallow graves, which attracted wolves and coyotes.

One legend claims that the town undertaker, a man known as "Black Peter," did an impressive job at his "seemingly endless task" during the epidemic, making the rounds of houses each morning with a cart on which he loaded the dead, sometimes finding whole families struck down by the disease. However, there were so many bodies that the mayor eventually told Peter there was no money or whiskey left to pay him for his services. So Peter propped a corpse on the mayor's front door, and when the man opened it the next morning, the body collapsed onto him. Within hours, the town had found the money to pay Peter to bury the bodies.[22]

While very likely apocryphal, the story illustrates the desperation of those left alive during cholera epidemics. Fear of touching the dead bodies infected with cholera was so intense, and the number of corpses so great, that burial became rushed by necessity. Mass graves were an unfortunate but pragmatic solution to the problem.

## SAN ANTONIO, 1866

Once cholera victims were buried, regardless of the location or their families' wishes, the bodies had to stay there for years, if not decades, and often forever. A corpse infected by cholera was considered dangerous long after the soul it once housed had departed. When cholera struck San Antonio for the first time in fifteen years, in 1866, it killed 292 people, and the city used an emergency fund of $144 to pay for their burial.[23] However, the First Battalion, Seventh Infantry Regiment (white) fled San Antonio for Medina, where they soon discovered that all their precautions against the disease had been useless when a cholera outbreak hit their ranks. Being so far outside the city, this left them to bury their own dead.

In the U.S. War Department's *Report on Epidemic Cholera*, published the following year, it listed sixty-four deaths of soldiers from cholera "at and near San Antonio, Texas" in September 1866 alone, plus five additional deaths with cholera-like symptoms, while there were only two deaths from "all other diseases."[24] The bodies were buried in a mass grave on the banks of the Medina River. The San Antonio Genealogical and Historical Society marks the "reported" site[25] as somewhere to the southeast of the Applewhite Road Bridge.[26]

When the San Antonio National Cemetery opened in 1868, many bodies of soldiers were removed from their graves in the surrounding area and reinterred in the military cemetery. However, this did not include cholera

After the 1866 cholera outbreak in San Antonio, it became obvious the city needed a hospital. The Sisters of Charity of the Incarnate Word opened St. Mary's Infirmary on December 3, 1869. The number of patients quickly exceeded the space available, and in 1874, building commenced on the much larger Santa Rosa Infirmary, pictured here around 1884. *The Heritage Center, Sisters of Charity of the Incarnate Word.*

victims. A U.S. Senate document from the time reveals that at least fifty bodies were left in the ground, "they being deaths from cholera and not sufficiently decomposed for removal with safety."[27] The military, like civilians, was terrified of spreading cholera by touching or moving victims' remains. Even in 1911, well after the cause of cholera was discovered, U.S. military law required victims of the disease to remain buried for two years before reinterment.[28] It seems the bodies in Medina were, in fact, never moved to the San Antonio National Cemetery and remain there in a now-lost unmarked mass grave.

## Fredericksburg, 1846

Other mass graves of cholera victims also remain unmarked, although some towns have worked to change this. In 1945, residents of Fredericksburg embarked on a beautification project for Der Stadt Friedhof (The City Cemetery) in honor of the centennial of the town's founding. A series of articles in the *Fredericksburg Standard* noted that hundreds of early settlers had died from cholera, but "the survivors were too weak and ill to properly mark the graves,"[29] and any markers that were placed on the graves had been lost in the ensuing century.[30] By 1975, the paper reported that the "large common graves" of the cholera victims were by then "enclosed with a rock ledge."[31] In 2011, local churches organized volunteers to rebuild the rock wall, which had evidently fallen into disrepair.[32]

# NEW BRAUNFELS, 1845–46

One town has even bigger plans. In the middle of New Braunfels Cemetery, what appears to be a large and unused expanse of land is actually a mass grave of early settlers, most of whom probably died of cholera in the 1845–46 epidemic; however, the Sophienburg Museum and Archives found the causes listed in the death records often sounded more like guesses based on symptoms and included convulsions, spinal meningitis, "mucus fever, bilious fever, dysentery, blood poisoning, and yellow fever."[33] In 2010, the New Braunfels City Council approved the Historic Preservation Plan for Municipal Cemeteries, which included marking the mass grave in New

Large stone blocks mark one corner of the mass grave in New Braunfels Cemetery, next to a sign explaining the plans for a memorial park on the site (as of 2022). *Author's collection.*

Braunfels Cemetery.[34] As of 2020, the Field of Graves Memorial project design included new trees, monuments, footpaths and seating for visitors to the cemetery, meant to give the memorial a meditative feel.

An excerpt from the writings of early settler Hermann Seele is planned for one stone pillar. Seele was in the area during the 1845–46 cholera outbreak and saw the horrors it wrought: "Only a few of the dead could be placed in coffins because of the lack of boards. In the summer as many as three—wrapped in canvas or blankets—were transported together every morning by a teamster in the employ of the society to the cemetery, where they were buried in a prescribed manner by the appointed gravediggers."[35]

As of 2022, the mass grave is marked on each corner by large stone blocks, and the project is ongoing. Hopefully, the cholera victims buried in New Braunfels Cemetery will soon have a fitting memorial.

# 3

# INFLUENZA

B arely one hundred years before the 2020 COVID-19 pandemic, countries around the world faced a similar problem. The 1918 influenza (once known as the Spanish flu) pandemic killed on such an unimaginable scale that it simply resulted in too many bodies for most places to handle. The *El Paso Herald* reported on the lack of even the most basic necessities for standard burials:

> *Grim evidence that influenza is taking heavy toll among the poorer classes in the lower valley was furnished Saturday morning when a wagon load of crude pine box coffins was delivered at the county storehouse, in the basement of the courthouse. The coffins were the first part of an order of 30, arranged by purchasing agent Joseph A. Escajeda. They will be used for emergency calls from the neighborhood of Fabens and the Island, where deaths at times have come faster than coffins could be supplied.*[36]

When there are more corpses than coffins, even in a time before cremation was standard and a crematorium always relatively close by, one still has to deal with the bodies. During the 1918 influenza pandemic, this often meant resorting to mass graves.

This dilemma was not limited to Texas. Mass graves known or suspected to be the final resting places of influenza victims have been found in areas as far afield as Alaska, Pennsylvania, Samoa, New Zealand, the United Kingdom and dozens of other locations.

## Waco, 1918

Waco was hit just as hard by the rampaging virus. According to the city's official website, Greenwood Cemetery holds a mass grave of influenza victims.[37] A 2014 report by the *Waco Tribune* notes that the grave was located in the area previously used as the "pauper cemetery on the Earle Street side of Greenwood."[38] However, there does not appear to be any information on its specific location. Like so many from the period, the influenza victims in Waco lie in an unmarked grave.[39]

It seems that, both in Texas and the rest of the world, people agreed that it was better to forget the tragedy that led to such a high death toll and subsequent breakdown of funereal norms. In the first major academic book on the 1918 pandemic, not published until 1976, University of Texas, Austin professor Alfred Crosby wrote of his astonishment at this decision: "One searches for explanations for the odd fact that Americans took little notice of the pandemic and then quickly forgot whatever they did notice."[40] In Waco, if you want to visit the mass grave of the victims of the 1918 influenza pandemic, at best you can make an educated guess on the location, somewhere along Earle Street.

Most notable for being a segregated cemetery, with the sections for Black burials and white burials divided by a fence as late as 2016, Greenwood Cemetery in Waco is also home to an unmarked grave of victims of the 1918 influenza pandemic. *Author's collection.*

# 4

# TORNADOES

By tradition, Texas is considered part of "Tornado Alley," but in actuality, most of the state is to the south and west of where the U.S. experiences the bulk of its tornado activity. As of 2022, there hasn't been a confirmed F5 tornado in the state in twenty-five years, since the 1997 Jarrell Tornado became the tenth-deadliest in Texas history.

The deadliest tornado the state has ever seen occurred in Waco in 1953. It appears that, thankfully, none of the 114 people killed ended up in a mass grave. The same cannot be said for victims of the second- and third-deadliest tornadoes: the Goliad Tornado of 1902 and the Rocksprings Tornado of 1927, respectively.

## THE 1902 GOLIAD TORNADO

Although it would be decades before the United States adopted the Fujita Scale for measuring tornadoes, the Goliad Tornado of 1902 is estimated to have been an F4, meaning winds of 207–260 miles per hour. While contemporary accounts of who died where and in what number vary, the final death toll is agreed to be 114—strangely, the same number killed in the 1953 Waco Tornado. But because that later storm resulted in 597 people injured to Goliad's 250, Waco is considered the "deadlier" tornado.[41] But Goliad in 1902 was no modern city, which meant the dead and injured added up to a shocking 27 percent casualty rate in the small town.[42]

In 1978, the Texas Historical Commission erected Marker Number 2207 to commemorate the storm. While accurate in the particulars, it is missing a feel of the absolute horror of the event for the survivors:

> *A cyclone, considered one of the two most disastrous in Texas history, struck Goliad on Sunday, May 18, 1902. The twister touched down on the south side of the San Antonio River at 3:35 p.m. Sounding like a heavily loaded freight train, the storm ripped a mile long, half-mile wide path across the northwest section of town, destroying over 100 homes and leaving an official death toll of 114. At least 50 members of a black Methodist church died when their sanctuary was razed. After the disaster, the Goliad County Courthouse served as a temporary hospital and morgue.*[43]

At the other extreme, contemporary newspaper accounts seemed to revel in the gory details of the suffering and death. A day after the tragedy, the *Courier-Journal* of Louisville, Kentucky, ran a front-page story on the tornado under the extremely to-the-point headline: "DEATH." Subheads went into more detail on the carnage, including "Victims Torn Limb from Limb or Crushed by Falling Walls" and "Victims Torn to Pieces by the Winds of Death."

After such evocative introductions to the tragedy at Goliad, the copy could deliver nothing less than the most sensational descriptions of the storm.

> *The force of the wind was fearful. Strong and substantial structures were swept away in the short space of a few seconds, and the unfortunate inmates were hurried about and then pinioned beneath tons upon tons of debris, some enduring the most excruciating pain and suffering untold agonies, others being killed so quickly that it is doubtful if they knew the cause of their fate.*
>
> *Others were picked up by the wind and hurled against trees, houses and fences with a force that tore them limb from limb and then left them dying, mutilated, and battered beyond recognition, even by their own loved ones, who were anxiously searching the ruins in the hope of finding some of the missing in time to render such aid as was in their power with the means at hand.*[44]

On May 21, the *Houston Post* printed an interview with D.T. Forbes, a railroad superintendent who was in charge of a relief train for Goliad. "I remember seeing a man with his head entirely cut off from the body, each

The First United Methodist Church of Goliad was demolished by the 1902 tornado. The congregation rebuilt the church within a year, using wood from the original building. *Goliad County Historical Commission.*

laying within a few inches of the other. In some instances, the sights were too repulsive to bear description."[45] If a decapitated body was not too repulsive to mention in the newspaper, one dreads to think what horrific incidences Mr. Forbes thought wise to withhold from the readership.

The aftermath of the storm meant the victims were unable to receive traditional burials. Many of the 114 dead were placed in a hastily dug trench at Lott Cemetery with no funeral services.[46] The cemetery's historical marker records, "After a tornado in 1902 destroyed Goliad's Fannin Street Methodist Episcopal Church and the surrounding neighborhood, several dozen victims…were interred in a communal grave along the Lott Cemetery's Eastern Boundary."[47] There is also a small memorial stone, erected in the town's more centrally located Sarpenter Cemetery in 2002—the centennial of the storm. It reads "In Remembrance of the May 18, 1902 Tornado Victims."[48]

# THE 1927 ROCKSPRINGS TORNADO

Twenty-five years later, the third-deadliest tornado in Texas history touched down near Rocksprings. Meteorologist J.H. Jarboe's report of the destruction recorded that when it hit the town, the tornado caused unbelievable damage: "The storm that occurred in Edwards and Real Counties on April 12, probably surpassed any previous record for this section of Texas. This tornado first made its appearance on the Edwards Plateau, in the north-central portion of Edwards County, where it hit and practically destroyed the town of Rocksprings, taking a toll of 72 lives and injuring 200 more. About 235 residences and business buildings were destroyed."[49]

The scale of the destruction is even starker considering that Rocksprings had only 247 buildings to begin with.[50] The town was erased from the face of the earth in the freakiest of freak storms. Not only did it surpass contemporary records, but no tornado activity in that area has come

## Tornado-Swept Town Starts Rebuilding

(By Pacific & Atlantic)

**WITH 47 IDENTIFIED DEAD** and many unidentified, Rocksprings, Texas, town flattened by tornado, today is turning to rehabilitation. Led by Herbert Reddy, Red Cross executive, first attempts were under way to rebuild the village. Five were killed in Oklahoma in storm which swept parts of that state. This picture gives you a graphic idea of the force of the Rocksprings storm. It shows sheet iron wrapped like paper around stripped tree. **(Other picture on page 28)**

Newspapers across the country published images of the terrible destruction in Rocksprings after the 1927 tornado. This picture in the *New York Daily News* shows "sheet iron wrapped like paper around [a] stripped tree." New York Daily News.

close to it since.[51] Meteorologists viewed the track from an airplane and estimated the twister was a mile wide. But it came out of nowhere and caught the town unprepared.

The power of the storm was astonishing. One witness reported seeing a house lifted up by the wind and thrown into another building across the street, demolishing both. A concrete building exploded. Once the winds stopped, a fire broke out that burned down two of the few structures left standing. The town had been transformed into a pile of debris, with the cries of the trapped and dying cutting through the night. Locals who had escaped unscathed rushed to their aide, but outside assistance was needed.

In order to call for help, Gladys Laurie (sometimes spelled Lowrey), a telephone operator, and Foster Owens, a telephone lineman, drove out into the night looking for a telephone wire that was still standing. They found one about a mile away, and, in the pouring rain, Owens climbed the pole and spliced the wire to the test telephone set he used for his job. One hundred miles away, a switchboard operator answered.[52]

Even once the outside world knew to send help, it proved difficult. Rocksprings's isolated, out-of-the-way location, thirty-five miles from the nearest railroad track[53] and sixty miles from the closest large town,[54] along with recent rains that made some roads impassable, resulted in delays to the lifesaving assistance it was desperate for.[55]

Almost every citizen of Sonora who was physically capable of assisting set off for Rocksprings when they learned about the destruction. One volunteer, Sam Thomas, wrote to his mother with details of the horrors the tornado left behind: "It was the most terrible thing I ever saw. I couldn't imagine wind could do such a thing.…There were dead people all stacked up in one of the banks…it was terrible.…Some of the people had big pieces of lumber through them, and they were killed in most every way."[56]

Of the estimated seventy-four fatalities caused by the tornado, most were buried by loved ones in Rocksprings Cemetery, although this was complicated by the fact that the town had no undertaker, there were not enough coffins available locally and a layer of rock necessitated the use of dynamite to blast open holes for the graves. Not all bodies were claimed, however. The cemetery has a small stone reading "Unknown—16 Graves." This is the marker for those victims who were unable to be identified and were buried in a mass grave. Based on contemporary reporting by the *Vernon Weekly Record*, it is likely that many of those who went to their grave with no names were Mexican or of Mexican descent.[57]

The cemetery's Historical Marker Number 4328, erected in 1989 by the Texas Historical Commission, mentions the tragedy but does not draw attention to the group burial, noting, "Among the more than one thousand graves are those of victims of a devastating tornado which struck the town on April 12, 1927."[58]

## THE 1927 GARLAND TORNADO

One other tornado, well outside the top ten most deadly in Texas history, also resulted in a mass grave that deserves mention. At Mills Cemetery in Garland, a single tombstone lists the names and birthdates of five members of the Smiley family, followed by the line "All died May 9, 1927." With no information on how they died included, a local legend sprang up, which proliferates on the internet to this day.[59]

It's said that patriarch Charles Smiley was a cruel man, and on that day, he got so angry that he murdered his whole family. Then, perhaps in a fit of remorse, he died by suicide.[60] Murder- and cemetery-related urban legends always need to have a ghost thrown in as well, and the Smiley mass grave is no different. The restless spirit of Charles Smiley is supposed to walk the cemetery at night in an angry rage. And if you lie on the family's grave at midnight on Halloween, they say you will feel Charles's arms wrap around you as he tries to pull you into the ground to join him.[61]

The story checks many local legend boxes, but as you can probably tell, it's not true. As research by Texas cemetery historian Tui Snider proves, the family died in a tornado that ripped through Garland in the middle of the night on May 9, 1927. Five of the seven members of the family were killed and two others injured.[62] But the natural fear that mass graves provoke—and, in this case, the creepy juxtaposition between the last name Smiley and brutal murder—resulted in an urban legend that the poor victims, especially father Charles, do not deserve.

# 5

# HURRICANES

E ven with advanced early warning systems, 24/7 news coverage and alerts sent to every cellphone, hurricanes can still result in mass casualty events and hundreds of millions of dollars in property damage. For Texans in the early twentieth century, without the benefit of all of that lifesaving information, even a small hurricane was dangerous. When the big ones hit, they caused more death and destruction than most people could comprehend.

## THE 1900 GALVESTON HURRICANE

The storm that struck Galveston on September 8, 1900, remains, to this day, the greatest natural disaster in U.S. history. The hurricane dropped nine inches of rain on the city in twenty-four hours, a record at the time. It is estimated the winds were blowing at speeds of 120 miles per hour or more. A fifteen-foot storm surge left the entire island underwater. In a time before flood mitigation efforts, Galveston became a death trap.

What little the islanders could have done to prepare, they saw no need to. First-person accounts record that there was no sign a bad storm was coming, let alone one that would top the record books for more than a century. But once the hurricane made its presence known, the destruction was swift and total.

Galveston reporter Richard Spillane made it to Houston two days after the storm and told the world about the complete and total destruction the hurricane left in its wake:

> *By 3 o'clock the waters of the Gulf and Bay met, and by dark, the entire city was submerged. The flooding of the electric light plant and the gas plants left the city in darkness. To go up on the streets was to court death. The wind was then at cyclonic velocity, roofs, cisterns, portions of buildings, telegraph poles and walls were falling, and the noise of the wind and the crashing of ill doings were terrifying in the extreme. The wind and waters rose steadily from dark until 5 o'clock Sunday morning. During all this time the people of Galveston were like rats in a trap....To leave a house was to drown. To remain was to court death in the wreckage.*[63]

The terror of those who survived the storm is clear from their accounts, but once the winds died down and the waters receded, they faced a new problem. Thousands and thousands of corpses covered the island. It is almost beyond comprehension how many dead bodies lay wherever one looked.

It is still not known exactly how many people died in the 1900 storm, but it may have been into the low five figures. Paul Lester, author of *The Great Galveston Disaster: Containing a Full and Thrilling Account of the Most Appalling Calamity of Modern Times*, which was published that year, put the numbers in perspective for contemporary Americans based on current events: "In the brief space of 12 hours more persons lost their lives than were killed during a year of the war between the British and the Boers or during a year and a half of our war in the Philippines."[64]

In his introduction to Paul Lester's book on the tragedy, eyewitness Richard Spillane—the Galveston reporter who first made it to Houston and informed the world how bad the situation on the island was—wrote:

> *How many lives were sacrificed to the storm King will never be known. The census taken in June showed that Galveston had a population of 38,000. Outside the city limits on Galveston Island there were 1,600 persons living. The dead in the city exceeded 5,000. Of the 1,600 living outside the city limits, 1,200 were lost. This frightful mortality—75 percent—outside the city is explained by the fact that most of the people there lived in frail structures and had no places of comparative safety to take refuge in. In the mainland district swept by the storm, at least 100 persons perished. It is safe, therefore, to state that at least 7,000 lives were lost.*[65]

His estimate was probably not far off, although on the lower end. Today, estimates put the death toll at anywhere between six thousand and twelve thousand.

While the whole island was affected, some areas got hit by the storm even worse than others. Richard Spillane writes: "The full energy of wind and water were directed upon that portion of the city between the Gulf and the Broadway Ridge. Of the lives lost in the city, 90% were in the district named."[66] While the rest of the island was decimated, that section of Galveston was obliterated.

It was the same when it came to individual families. While no one on the island managed to get through the storm without some kind of loss, be it property or financial or personal, Spillane recounts how "in some cases whole families were blotted out, in others the strong perished and the weak survived. Of the various branches of one family, 42 were killed, while in one household 13 out of a total of 15 were lost."[67] Whole families, multiple generations, were wiped out; entire lineages were destroyed in half a day.

The force of the wind and water washed many corpses out to sea, but they soon returned to land to join those that had never gone anywhere in the first place. Paul Lester's book includes an account from an unnamed eyewitness. Lester says it was written almost immediately after the storm hit. The eyewitness tried to explain the volume of bodies suddenly covering the island. "In a radius of approximately 20 miles from Virginia point, the center of railroad relief operations, up to late this afternoon more than 700 corpses had been washed ashore or picked up from the mainland. Hitchcock, Clear Creek, Texas City, Virginia point, Seabrook, Alvin, Dickinson and half a dozen other points midway between Houston and Galveston compose one vast morgue."[68]

Perhaps a morgue wasn't the right comparison, though. Morgues are organized, with the dead neatly filed away. Spillane had a slightly different comparison. "Beneath these masses of broken buildings, in the streets, in the yards, in dense corners, in cisterns, in the bay, far out across the waters on the mainland shores, everywhere, in fact, were corpses. Galveston was a veritable charnel house."[69]

When Richard Spillane made it to Houston on September 10, before he alerted the newspapers, he sent a telegram to the White House. Even in that to-the-point missive, where every word counted, he deemed it important to tell President William McKinley that "when I left this morning the search for bodies had begun. Corpses were everywhere."[70] To fully understand what Galveston had been through and what they were about to face, as well as the amount of assistance required immediately, it was necessary for people to understand: the dead were *everywhere*.

Paul Lester recorded the experiences of J.W.B. Smith and Clegg Stewart as they escaped from Galveston to Houston. The voyage was almost too grim to be believed: "In every direction crossing the Bay they saw the feet of corpses sticking out of the water. Upon reaching land they walked to Hitchcock, Mr. Stewart's home, and found that 25 persons had lost their lives there, and that, in addition, 50 bodies that had floated ashore had been buried near there."[71]

In 1980, Bob Nesbitt of the Galveston and Texas History Center interviewed Hyman Block, a survivor of the 1900 storm who was a child at the time but whose memories of the event were vivid and horrible. Perhaps because of his age when the disaster occurred, in Block's version of events, the death and suffering have a veneer of the curiosity of a child. "I think Monday morning, I met Marion Levy and he said, 'Hyman, they tell me there is a lot of people who have been hurt and they haven't got enough room for them over at the undertaking establishment. Let's go over and see it.'"[72]

What their young eyes were about to see would stay with Hyman Block for all those decades. "In those days all of the express companies had these very high bins, I call them. They were about 10 or 15 feet high. They were built especially to carry loads of cotton samples. We got around to about a block away from J. Levy & Brothers. We saw four or five of those things stacked to the top with dead bodies and we got a breath of air and that is as far as I went. I went back home and Marion went home."[73] The sights and smells were unbearable.

Hyman Block was not the only one who could not bear to be near the piles of rotting corpses. The Galveston and Texas History Center's Marilee Neale interviewed storm survivors Henry J. Bettencourt and Margaret Rowan Bettencourt in 1972. Margaret recalled, "My oldest brother…he had a very weak stomach.…He couldn't stand to look at dead people.…So, my daddy was a Knight of Pythias, and all they, they all got together, they got their families together, and they sent, as soon as there was a train leave out of here, they sent all their families to Houston. And kept them over there until the, until they cleaned up here. Cleaned up in Galveston."[74]

Many women and children were sent away as soon as it was possible to leave Galveston. It was not just because the destruction and death turned people's stomachs, but because staying in the midst of so many putrefying bodies posed a very real and immediate threat to the living.

Cleaning up the island after the 1900 Galveston hurricane was a monumental task. A stereograph shows survivors searching for the bodies of victims in what the reverse of the card calls "an unparalleled scene of ruin and desolation." *New York Public Library*.

Another one of Paul Lester's unnamed eyewitnesses recorded how the people on the island begged outsiders for assistance: "Signal reports from men sent forward to Galveston Island to the relief parties on the mainland read: 60 dead bodies in one block. 600 corpses recovered and 400 more reported. People dying from injuries and sickness and for want of freshwater. Survivors threatened with starvation and disease. Doctors, nurses and freshwater needed at once."[75]

Over and over and over again in contemporary accounts, those writing draw attention to the astonishing number of dead. But one thing that is missing is the sense of tragedy, of the fact that they knew these people, these were their loved ones and neighbors. There would be time for mourning later. In an event that might be the closest real-life comparison to a zombie apocalypse, the dead had become a single, dangerous mass. And not just the corpses of humans, as one Houston paper explained: "So far the efforts of the searchers have necessarily been confined to the open places, and it will be sometime before the dead swept into the fields, the alleys and the dollies are gathered and laid away good. The city is one awful stench of decaying animal matter. Nearly every animal on the island was killed, and the thousands of human remains still scattered beneath the vast piles of debris add to the danger of the situation."[76]

Richard Spillane put this in stark terms: "To protect the living the dead had to be gotten rid of with all speed, for with corpses on every side, with carcasses by the thousands, and with a severe tropic sun to hasten decomposition, pestilence in its most terrible form threaten the living if the dead were not removed."[77]

As one would imagine, many of the men of Galveston were not anxious to get among the dead in the heat and stench and danger. A triumvirate of important citizens was put in charge of the island and introduced a form of martial law. The result: if being on the streets during the storm was to court death, being on the streets after the storm was to cart the dead. In his 1972 interview, Henry J. Bettencourt recalled: "all able-bodied men wasn't [sic] allowed on the street unless they were put to work. Cleaning up the city, moving bodies and all that."[78]

Another anonymous eyewitness whose account was recorded by Paul Lester spoke about those forced to deal with the bodies: "Chief of Police Ketchum…began to swear in hundreds of special policemen to rescue the wounded, feed the living and convey the dead to a hundred different morgues." The account continues: "The stench from the dead by Monday morning was unbearable. The triumvirate ruling the city pressed citizens into service to take the dead out in barges and bury them in the Gulf. The soldiers impressed into service, at the point of the bayonet, every wagon that came along and every negro to assist."[79]

Meteorologist John D. Blagden, who had been temporarily assigned to the Galveston Weather Bureau and is one of the most reliable eyewitnesses of the storm, wrote to his family in Minnesota about the amount of effort it took to remove the bodies. "Hundreds are busy day and night clearing away debris and recovering the dead. It is awful. Every few minutes a wagonload of corpses passes by on the street.[80]

The boat *Brunswick* brought more updates from the island to Houston, printed in one of the newspapers there. This new information made it clear that while some men in Galveston fought the labors being forced on them, the reality of the situation soon brought them into line: "Three undertaking establishments are all being utilized as morgues, and a fourth morgue was opened in a large building on the Strand. Some of the draymen at first refused to haul more than one body at a time, demanding the price for a full load for each trip. On Sunday evening, however, the few who made this demand agreed to bring as many bodies as their carts would hold."[81]

Hyman Block was able to add more personal details to these sickening tasks, as he told his interviewer what happened to his brother: "He was impressed. He was made a deputy marshal and given a bottle of whiskey and his job was at the Mensing Building.…By that time, they were still

**BURYING THE DEAD BY MOONLIGHT.**

Last Monday night, between the hours of 9 p. m. and 1 a. m., sixty-five bodies of storm victims were buried near the bay at Virginia Point, where they had washed ashore. The sketch above represents a burial scene in which a Post artist assisted in putting away the dead.

An artist for the *Houston Post* helped bury sixty-five bodies on the beach two days after the storm, and later, the paper published his drawing of the grim task. A Connecticut newspaper, *The Journal*, described—but did not publish—the image, calling it "rather ghastly." Houston Post.

continuing their efforts to identify bodies. As fast as they were bringing bodies in, they were bringing them into Mensing's and stacking them on the floor."[82]

Perhaps instinctively, the survivors of the hurricane at first attempted to bury all those thousands of victims. But it quickly became clear that "to bury the dead was a physical impossibility," as Richard Spillane wrote.

Paul Lester records an anonymous source's recollection of how it dawned on those in charge that even mass graves would not be able to deal with the number of bodies that had to be disposed of. "A terrible stench permeates the atmosphere. It comes from the bodies of a thousand unburied dead festering in the debris, that cannot be removed for weeks on account of the paucity of laborers. Every tide brings scores back to the shore. During the early part of yesterday trenches were dug and the bodies thrown into them, but it soon became an impossibility to bury all."[83]

An unnamed newspaper cited in *The Great Galveston Disaster* reported, "It became apparent that it would be impossible to bury the dead, even in trenches, and arrangements were made to take them to sea."[84]

Therefore, after a long, horrible day of mass burials, digging further mass graves was rejected in favor of other attempts to dispose of the corpses. They would be equally unsuccessful.

First, the decision was made to give the dead mass burials at sea. This seemed logical and expedient, what with Galveston being surrounded by water and plenty of barges available to tow the bodies out to sea.

The reality was less than ideal.

Paul Lester recorded that some went back to digging mass graves after burial at sea failed. "It was found to be impossible to send bodies to sea for burial. The water receded so far, however, that it was possible to dig trenches, and bodies were being buried where found. Debris covering bodies was being burned where it could be done safely."[85]

Hyman Block's memories line up with this report almost exactly: "Well, you know the story. They took these bodies and put them on barges and they took them out to the ocean and the ocean brought them back to them. That's when they gave up and started burning all of the debris wherever it was."

According to Lester, "Too much time was lost in consigning the dead to the sea, and the workers were compelled by the exigencies of the situation to pile the corpses where found and cremate them as well as this could be done."[86]

Once both mass ground burial and mass sea burial were ruled out, those on Galveston resorted to something that was many decades from public acceptance in the United States: they cremated the bodies. J.C. Roberts traveled from Houston to Galveston and was one of the first from off the island to arrive after the storm. His account sums up how a population that would have railed against cremation only days earlier set to it with all speed: "A description of the burning of the dead and the burial at sea is beyond reproduction. All sentiment is at an end. It has become a matter of self-protection and in order to avoid pestilence rapid disposal of the corpses is necessary." There was no ignoring the sight or smell of the mass cremation. Roberts's account continues: "Bonfires are burning all over the city. They are the funeral of a thousand festering corpses cast back up on the shore at high tide yesterday. Cremation has become a necessity."[87]

On September 9, 2000, the Place of Remembrance monument (located on Seawall Boulevard near Forty-Eighth Street) was dedicated to the memory of those who died in the 1900 Galveston storm. The ten-foot-tall bronze sculpture was created by fourth-generation Galvestonian artist David Moore. *Jim Evans/Wikimedia Commons (Creative Commons Attribution-Share Alike 4.0 International license).*

Manager of the Dallas Electric Company W. McGrath also made his way to Galveston, and after seeing the situation was not only for immolating the bodies but also for state-sponsored cremation: "The only way to prevent an epidemic that will practically depopulate the island is to burn the bodies of the dead. The governor of Texas should call an extra session of the legislature and appropriate a million or half a million, or whatever amount is needed. The situation must be taken intelligently in hand to save the state from a possible epidemic."[88]

Before the town resorted to cremation, many bodies were buried where they were found by anyone who was physically capable of doing the deed. It is thus impossible to know the number of mass graves of hurricane victims hidden beneath the feet of modern Galveston residents. Contemporary accounts indicate that many mass graves lined the beaches of the island. Paul Lester writes: "Volunteer gangs continue their work of hurry burial of the corpses they find on the shores of Galveston Island, at the many neighboring points where fatalities attended the storm. It will probably be many days, yet, however, before all the floating bodies have found nameless graves."

# The Hurricane of 1919

While often overshadowed by the record-breaking destruction and devastation of the 1900 storm, the Hurricane of 1919, also known as the Florida Keys Hurricane, was the deadliest storm to hit the Coastal Bend of Texas.

The Corpus Christi Weather Bureau's contemporaneous account of the hurricane describes the violence of the wind and the extremely high water level, which it reported was the highest in living memory. Many residents of the city had been informed of the danger and the need to flee their homes only shortly before the storm hit, so most did not have sufficient time to evacuate.

Perhaps because the 1900 storm that destroyed Galveston was still very much in living memory, some sources from the time play down how bad the 1919 hurricane was. Many people died in that storm, and more lost their houses or faced other damage. When viewed in isolation, it was a terrible and destructive storm. But it can never be viewed in anything other than a favorable comparison to Galveston. And, to be fair, those hit by the 1919 storm do seem to have been lucky when it came to the number of casualties, considering how strong the storm was. Today, it is estimated to have been a Category 3 storm, with winds of 115 miles per hour, when it hit Corpus Christi on September 14. The storm surge was almost twelve feet in the center of the city, and the event caused the equivalent of more than $300 million in property damage.

Most of the casualties, however, occurred in the North Beach area. As the worst hurricanes in the previous decade had never come as far south as Corpus Christi, many who lived in the area had a false sense of security. This storm not only reached them but also was strong enough to wash away homes—with the residents still inside.

On September 17, 1919, the *El Paso Times* quoted the head of the local relief committee in Corpus Christi, who predicted, "considering the intensity and extent of the storm, the loss of lives is doubtless small, probably not to exceed 100." However, the same article reported that the National Guard had informed the governor "that at least 1,000 bodies were strewn along the Texas coast as a result of the hurricane."[89] The contemporary report by the Corpus Christi Weather Bureau estimated that "the destruction of life amounted to between 300 and 400 people in Corpus Christi and a considerable number from places north of Corpus Christi Bay were lost."[90]

By September 21, the *San Angelino Evening Standard* reported the death toll had reached 386. At least, that was the number of victims found and buried a week after the storm hit. While the paper predicted only a few more bodies would be discovered, it said there would be "no let-up" in the search.[91]

The National Weather Service records that the official death toll was 284 people, although a person was only "officially" recorded as deceased if their body had been positively identified. Most of the bodies had not been identified before being quickly buried on the beaches where they were found. This means the real death toll is thought to be in the range of 600 to 1,000.

Texas Historical Commission Marker Number 12186 gives one of the more detailed and evocative descriptions found on any historical marker, allowing the reader to put themselves in the difficult position of those who survived the hurricane and were faced with its aftermath.

*Over the next few days, more than 200 people worked to rescue survivors and retrieve the dead. Bodies were taken to the West Portland schoolhouse on this site. Identifying the remains proved difficult; the bodies were broken, covered in oil, and in some cases whole families had perished, leaving no one to identify them. The remains were weighed on a cotton scale and taken almost a mile back toward the beach where they were found. They were laid to rest in a mass grave dug with a slip scraper. More than 30 separate graves were dug from Indian Point near Portland to a spot about 20 miles up Nueces Bay. Some of the larger graves measured 1400 feet wide and 3200 feet long. Evidence indicates that all the bodies were moved to Rose Hill Cemetery in Corpus Christi and to other sites about a month later. The official death toll was 284; estimates place the actual number, including those lost at sea, at about 1,000....This gravesite and the others serve as a reminder of the power of the elements.*[92]

During emergency relief efforts after a disaster like the 1919 hurricane, mass graves can be both necessary and the best decision at the time. But once the immediate danger is passed, these mass burial solutions can be reassessed. Sometimes, if the identities of those in mass graves are known, their families will ask that their remains be exhumed for reburial elsewhere. This is what happened to those in one mass grave in 1919, as Texas Historical Commission Marker Number 12181 explains:

*On Monday morning the sun rose on a scene of terrible destruction. Though the official death toll was 284, estimates place the actual number, including those lost at sea, at one thousand. In the ensuing days, the survivors worked together to rebuild their homes, rescue the injured and bury the dead in mass graves, some containing more than fifty bodies, using farm implements as undertaking tools. A month later the bodies were removed to Rose Hill Cemetery in Corpus Christi and other sites as requested by friends and family members.*[93]

Many unknown victims ended up in another mass grave at Rose Hill. There, the American Red Cross placed a large boulder "in memory of the unidentified dead who lost their lives in the storm of Sept. 14, 1919."[94]

# II

# THIS LAND IS MY LAND

The story most schoolchildren in Texas (and, indeed, in all other states) grew up learning about the colonization of the United States was one of "settlers" searching for the American Dream and "Manifest Destiny" that gave a noble and inevitable sense of purpose to the invasion of the continent.

Native American tribes living on the land that eventually became Texas—including the Comanche, Tonkawa, Lipan Apache, Kiowa, Wichita, Caddo, Atakapa and Karankawa—had a very different view of these invaders. They watched as their lands were encroached on, then taken away in treaties, which were then broken. It did not matter if they were a "friendly" tribe to the colonizers or hostile, in the end, they would lose their way of life and their homes.

Just as any Texan would today if a stranger tried to take over their house room by room, the Native tribes fought back. These clashes do not have good guys or bad guys. They were complicated encounters between groups, both of which wanted to live and flourish and found themselves in conflict with those who were in their way. Atrocities were a sad fact of life. Long before Texas was a state or a republic, colonizers and Native Americans found themselves in violent conflict.

# 6
# FORT ST. LOUIS, 1688

To reduce two hundred years of European colonization to a few broad strokes, the English settled the East Coast of the present-day United States and the Spanish settled the West. The French were left to walk, as it were, the dividing line between them, traveling the Mississippi River from the Great Lakes region to the Gulf of Mexico in order to claim more territory for themselves.

One of the first of these men was René-Robert Cavelier, Sieur de La Salle, commonly known as La Salle. In 1685, near present-day Victoria, he founded the settlement that has come to be known as Fort St. Louis with about three hundred other colonizers.

La Salle was not a great leader, and everything seemed to go wrong at the fort. Food was scarce. Worse still, the colonists found themselves stranded when their ship ran aground. Numbers at the fort decreased as people died from disease, overwork and the elements; deserted; or set out on further expeditions. Within months, the fort's population was reduced by half.[95] La Salle himself left the fort to search for the mouth of the Mississippi River in 1687. It was the beginning of the end for the remaining colonizers.

La Salle was not concerned with making friends with the Karankawas and ordered they be shot on sight. There were skirmishes in which both colonizers and Native Americans were killed. When the local tribe learned La Salle was gone and there was no united front among the remaining twenty colonizers—the number included women and children—they saw an opportunity to take back their land. They offered warmer relations, then struck.

Only one boy who survived the attack was still alive to tell the tale years later. He had been taken and lived with the Karankawas. Nine or ten years old at the time the fort was set upon, Jean-Baptiste Talon laid out his recollection of what happened at Fort St. Louis to an interviewer in 1698.

> As the French were no longer on their guard, believing [the Karankawa] to be friends, these had little trouble slaughtering them all, except the said Jean-Baptiste Talon; two of his brothers, younger than he, named Robert and Lucien; their older sister, named Marie-Magdalene; and another young Parisian named Eustache Bremen. They were saved by some women, who touched with compassion by their youth, loaded them on their backs and carried them into their cabins while their husbands massacred the rest, after the said Talons had seen their mother fall before their eyes.[96]

A year after the attack, General Alonso de Leon and his men came across the remains of the fort. He wrote of the gruesome scene: "We found three dead bodies scattered over the plain. One of these, from the dress that still clung to the bones, appeared to be that of a woman. We took the bodies up, chanted mass with the bodies present, and buried them. We looked for the other dead bodies but could not find them; whence we supposed that they had been thrown into the creek and had been eaten by alligators, of which were many."[97]

Modern archaeologists have confirmed many of these details, including that the bodies were exposed to the elements for quite a while before being buried together in a mass grave.

# FORT PARKER, 1836

While the members of the Pilgrim Baptist Church in Illinois received permission to settle in Texas from the Mexican government, no one thought to ask the local Comanche and Kiowa tribes.

Arriving in Limestone County in 1833, the group, led by John Parker, built a fort and houses and began farming. It was a fraught period to arrive in Texas, and in 1836, the colonizers fled as the Mexican army headed in their direction. However, once they learned Santa Anna had surrendered, the Parkers returned to the fort.

Only weeks later, on May 19, 1836, a group of Comanches and Kiowas attacked Fort Parker. At first approaching waving a white flag, they spoke with Benjamin Parker, asking for meat and directions to good campgrounds. But when he returned to speak with them again, they killed him and bore down on the fort. Most of the colonizers were in the fields already, while others were able to flee. All told, the Natives killed five men and kidnapped five women and children.[98]

A large monument to Fort Parker, topped with life-size statues of a man, a woman and a child, is located in Groesbeck. Among the inscriptions is the following:

*Established by Illinois colonists in 1833*
—

*Three years later*
*At 8 o'clock A.M.*
*As the dew-drops glistened in the sun-rays—*
*"It fell"*
*By the hand of the Comanches.*

Located just yards away is a large stone slab covering the common grave of the five victims of the attack: John Parker, Benjamin F. Parker, Silas M. Parker, Samuel M. Frost and Robert Frost. The chosen burial site, under a large oak tree, was about one and a half miles from the fort and would form the basis of a cemetery where burials continue today.

## The Gotier Family Massacre, circa 1837

James Gotier (also spelled Goacher, Goucher and Gotcher) is most notable for receiving permission from the ayuntamiento of San Felipe in the early 1830s to build a road connecting that city and the settlements along the Colorado River near modern-day Bastrop. At the time, it was the only marked trail available to colonizers in the area.

The Gotier family made use of this trail themselves when they moved to Bastrop County in 1835. Having already been the first white settlers in Lee County (so it is said), they then built what is thought to be the first house in the county.

James planned on raising cattle and farming, but not long after they arrived, the five members of the family—James, his wife, his son-in-law and both of his sons—were killed by Native Americans. They were buried together in a single grave.

The imposing monument to Fort Parker settlers stands a dozen yards from the easily overlooked flat stone covering the common grave of the five men killed in an attack by members of the Comanche and Kiowa tribes in 1836. *Author's collection.*

While many accounts of deaths on the frontier have conflicting details, what is interesting about the Gotiers is that two official Texas Historical Markers disagree not only about how to spell their last name but also about the date the family was killed. A large stone, Marker Number 8154, dedicated to James lists him as a "Goucher" and is inscribed with a death date of November 26, 1836.[99] The marker for the trace he built, Number 9190, displays the name "Gotier" and records that the family was killed in 1837.[100]

## THE SURVEYORS' FIGHT, 1838

By the 1830s, colonizers of various nationalities had been in Texas long enough that the Native tribes knew signs of trouble. The most concerning was not a military force but the surveyors. Where surveyors came with their instruments, colonizers soon followed, and tribes lost their land. Following the Texas Revolution, many former soldiers held bounties for land promised to them by the new government. So surveyors were sent out.

In Navarro County, a surveying party of an estimated twenty-two to twenty-seven men (sources vary) set out in September 1838. In an eerie bit of foreshadowing, they first camped at the aforementioned Fort Parker, which had been attacked by Comanches just two years earlier and resulted in five men buried in a common grave. Almost exactly the same fate would befall the surveyors.

They knew the danger facing them. That summer, three men from another surveying party had been killed nearby. And the first-person account of Walter Lane, who wrote at length on the events, makes clear they were warned as soon as they reached their destination that concerned tribes would try to remove the group from their hunting grounds, one way or another. When a group of Kickapoos explained to the surveyors that if they stayed in the area Comanches and Ionies would kill them, Lane writes, "We thanked them for the information, but said that we were not afraid of the Ionies, and said if they attacked us we would clean them out, as they have nothing but bows and arrows anyway."

Nor were the surveyors in doubt of the reason they would almost certainly be attacked. Lane notes: "The Indians had no hostility towards us, but knew as we were surveying the land, that the white people would soon settle there and break up their hunting grounds, so they wanted to kill us for a double purpose—none would be left to tell on them, and it would deter others from coming into that section of country surveying."

Even Texas Historical Commission Marker Number 8271, erected in 1966, is clear that the men "fail[ed] to heed warning[s] to leave."[101]

Yet, the Texas Ranger Museum describes the situation very differently on its website, claiming the surveyors were "seemingly ignorant of their danger."[102] While perhaps a small quibble on its face, this example encapsulates how even when there is strong historical evidence of what occurred, it is often impossible to avoid giving in to tropes concerning conflicts between whites and Natives. In this case, it is clear the surveyors were aware of the danger they were in and that they were in it because they were facilitating the theft of land from tribes that had been there first and did not want to leave. They made the choice to stay, not because they did not believe they would be attacked but because they believed that when they were, it would be easy to kill the Natives.

The Battle of Battle Creek, also known as the Surveyors' Fight, or the Battle Creek Fight, took place on October 8, 1838. The definitive account of this deadly clash comes from survivor Walter P. Lane, who wrote extensively about it, including in his memoir. The morning of the fight, the group received one final warning, this time from two of their own, who needed a replacement compass and urged the rest of the surveyors not to set off until they returned with it.

These many warnings were still not heeded, and shortly after the surveyors set to work that day, they were attacked by the same Kickapoo who had told them to leave the area. Surrounded, the surveyors found cover in a ravine, where they tried unsuccessfully to repel the attack until nightfall. By then, many of the men were dead or wounded, and the rest tried to escape in the darkness. But as there was a full moon, the Kickapoo continued their assault when they saw the white men escaping.

Walter P. Lane was badly injured, and others were killed. The survivors carried on, leaving one man behind when he could not go on. Lane passed out and was almost left for dead. The remaining three men finally found some luck in their attempt to get to Fort Parker when a group of Kickapoo offered assistance, believing the men had been attacked not by their own tribe but by the revival Ionies. Then the trio of surveyors encountered the two men of their party who had left to get a working compass, and they were able to ride the rest of the way to the fort.

Once those at Fort Parker learned what had transpired, they returned to the scene of the clash. In an 1885 letter to historian James T. DeShields, who had requested an account of the fight from a very aged Lane, the latter wrote, "In two days after we got to Franklin, the people raised a company

The final resting place of the white casualties of the Surveyors' Fight is perhaps one of the loveliest mass graves in Texas: located on a flat plain near Dawson, under a large tree, marked by a classic white obelisk and enclosed by a wrought-iron fence. *Author's collection.*

and went to Battle Creek and buried bones of our men." In his memoirs, Lane details, "They found the bones of all our killed, the flesh having been stripped off by the wolves."[103] They buried the men in a single grave.

As Lane wrote to DeShields, the surveyor party, which would not listen to warnings, suffered a horrible number of casualties: "Summed up, 16 killed, seven escaped, five of whom were badly wounded."[104] However, it may have been even worse than that, as Lane might have forgotten the exact numbers in his old age. It's thought up to eighteen men could have been killed.

## MILAM PARK, 1838

While the Surveyors' Fight is by far the most infamous clash between Texian surveyors and Native Americans, it was not the only one. It was not even the only deadly encounter between the two groups in October 1838. On October 20, a mere twelve days after the Surveyors' Fight, a group of Comanches, possibly up to one hundred strong, attacked a much smaller party of surveyors near San Antonio. Sources cannot agree on how many Texians were killed, but it is placed at somewhere between two and five casualties.

The survivors quickly returned to San Antonio and raised the alarm. That same day, Captain Benjamin Franklin Cage led volunteers to find the Comanches and retaliate. However, they were also no match for the Native force once they found them. Three of Cage's men were killed before the group fled back toward San Antonio. Before making it to the city, five more Texians were dead at the hands of the Comanches. Another four were badly wounded.

The bodies of the eight dead men were buried together in a mass grave just outside San Antonio's Catholic cemetery. Today, it is located under Milam Park.

# BIRD CREEK, 1839

It was not necessary for an inciting incident to occur to result in violence between Texians and Native Americans. Inhabiting the same region was enough that, eventually, one side or the other would decide to attack. Even encountering one another on the Texas prairie by accident was enough to trigger a deadly chain of events, as it did in May 1839.

On May 25, Captain John Bird was escorting prisoners between Fort Milam and Fort Little River when they ran into a handful of Native Americans skinning a buffalo. Once at Fort Little River, Bird learned of other soldiers' recent run-ins with local tribes and decided to go looking for a fight. The next day, he set off with about thirty-five men.

The party soon encountered a group of Native Americans of comparable size, liked their odds and gave chase. But Bird and his men had fallen into a trap. After a lengthy pursuit, the Texians were surrounded by more than forty members of local Caddo, Kickapoo and Comanche tribes. Under heavy fire, the white men fled to the safety of a ravine. The Natives fell back and waited for reinforcements, which further swelled their ranks. Soon, Bird and his men were facing a force of two hundred.

Legend has it that while rallying his troops, Captain Bird was killed by an arrow to the heart that was shot from two hundred yards away. Four of his men also fell in the battle. But the fight was considered a victory for the Texians.

In a report written on May 31, 1839, Captain Nathan Brookshire outlined how the battle ended: "The Indians then separated into two bodies and marched off, throwing up into the air composition of something that had the appearance of lightning, which we supposed to be a signal for retreat. About 9 o'clock, we secreted our dead in the ravine, as well as possible, and took up a line of march down the ravine, in order to gain the timber, a distance of 3 miles, carrying off our wounded with us."

The men made it to Camp Nashville. After a brief recovery, they went back for the men they left behind. Brookshire wrote, "We will leave this place tomorrow [June 1] morning, together with a hundred of the citizens, for the battleground, to inter the dead and see what other discoveries we can make."[105]

Brookshire was good to his word, and Captain Bird and his men did receive a proper burial, even if they ended up in a mass grave. James T. DeShields (who, as previously mentioned, had also written to Walter P. Lane in 1885 asking for his recollections on the Surveyors' Fight) wrote about Bird Creek in *U.S. Magazine* and explained how the five fallen soldiers were laid to rest as one: "A huge coffin had been prepared, and into this uncouth receptacle all that was mortal of Capt. Bird and his unfortunate comrades was placed and sent back to the settlement for burial. The remains of the five men now repose side-by-side on the bank of Little River, near the site of old Fort Griffin."[106]

## THE WEBSTER MASSACRE, 1839

John Webster originally hailed from Virginia and migrated to Texas in 1837. After settling in Bastrop for a short time, he acquired a land grant near present-day Leander. But the area was still fully controlled by the Comanches. Undeterred, Webster set off with thirteen men; his wife, Dolly Webster; and their two young children.

After seeing evidence that Comanches were in the area, the group turned back, but either a broken axle on one of their wagons or a particularly dark night delayed their retreat. They made camp, circling the wagons in order to have some protection in case of hostilities.

It would not be enough. The next morning, the party found itself under attack. They were outnumbered, but it's not clear by how much. Virginia Webster, just three years old at the time, wrote an account many decades later and recalled the men of the group estimating there were three hundred Comanches surrounding them. Her obituary in the *Victoria Advocate* in 1927, however, increased this number to an incredible nine hundred.[107]

Victims of the Webster Massacre are said to be buried in Davis Cemetery in Leander. As well as the tomb and large slab memorial, a second, more elaborate marker located in the Old Town also commemorates the casualties, noting, "In death they rest together in one grave." *Author's collection.*

Indeed, almost every newspaper account of the massacre in the first few decades of the 1900s is written in a tone more appropriate for dime novel Westerns. And since many details, from the number of victims to the age and name of Victoria, differ in every account, it is hard to be sure of the facts.

However, what is clear is that all the men of the Webster party were killed (some accounts say this was fourteen men; others say upward of forty). Dolly and Virginia Webster, as well as the young boy Buster Webster, were kidnapped.[108]

Not all members of the Webster party were with the group that was attacked, some having been delayed by various errands. One was the surveyor John Harvey, who discovered a ghastly sight when he caught up with the group. In his memoirs, John Holland Jenkins, who as a boy lived in the Bastrop area at the same time as the Websters, wrote:

> *In a few days Harvey, knowing nothing of the fate of his party, went on to join them at Webster's, and came upon their skeletons lying in the*

*circle of 30 feet around the wagons. He returned in haste and made the report. Burleson immediately raised 50 or 60 men and hurried to the scene of carnage. A strange, unreal site of horror met our eyes. Only fleshless bones scattered around remains of a brave and courageous band of men. In absence of coffin, box, or even plank, we collected them into an old crate, which was found nearby, and buried them.*[109]

An account based on a 1904 interview with John W. Darlington, a laborer working for Webster who was also not traveling with the group when they were killed, records a different version of events that led to the discovering of the murdered party: "Shortly after the massacre some of the stock belonging to the Webster party came into the Hornsby settlement with Indian arrows sticking in their bodies. This alarmed the settlers and they immediately sent out a rescuing party to investigate the cause of this condition of the livestock. The rescuers found the bodies lying as described and they were all buried in one grave near the place of the massacre."[110]

Today, their grave is marked by a large gravestone in the small and unassuming Davis Cemetery in Leander.

## THE RIPLEY MASSACRE, 1841

Many of these clashes between Native Americans and those trying to colonize their land left behind mass graves, an unknown number of which have long been forgotten. Stumbling across one on the Texas frontier in the 1800s does not seem to have been at all shocking.

In 1917, W.D. Moore sent a diary that one of his relatives kept in 1847 to the *Southwestern Historical Quarterly* for publication. The entry for June 23, which is both preceded and followed by notes on crop hardiness and is written in the same tone, says in part: "We passed today the scene of an Indian massacre when 8 unfortunate members of the same family they buried in one common grave all the family were killed and scalped but three of father and two daughters the father was absent drinking whiskey at a neighboring grog shop the two daughters made their escape by hard running and good hiding the name of the family was Ripley."[111]

Texas Historical Marker Number 9849 gives more insight into what atrocity Moore's relative had stumbled upon. Ambrose and Rachel Ripley brought their family to Texas in 1837, settling in what is now Franklin County. Then, "On April 10, 1841, while Ripley was away, a band of

Indians attacked his farmstead, killing first his eldest son who was plowing in the field. Mrs. Ripley and five children were killed trying to reach a canebreak and one infant died when the house was burned."[112] (Note that the marker simply says Ambrose was "away," while the diarist claims he was "absent drinking.")

Because the area where they lived saw very few clashes with Native Americans, the Ripley Massacre had an outsized effect. A posse immediately murdered members of the first group of Native Americans they encountered, despite no evidence the victims had been involved in the killing of the Ripleys. The Ripley deaths also led to the support of stricter "anti-Indian policies" (as the marker puts it) and the creation of a local militia tasked with removing Native American tribes from the area, one way or another.

# PROFFITT, 1867

On July 17, 1867, three young men named Rice Carlton, Reuben Johnson and Patrick Proffitt set to work branding cattle near Fort Belknap. But a day that had been like so many others for the three young men suddenly turned deadly when they were attacked by a group of Native Americans. How many, from what tribe and what—if any—reason there was for a deadly ambush were unclear. The three men were rendered helpless, as their guns were on their horses and their horses had wandered off to graze. They were all killed while trying to get to their weapons.

In 1990, the Texas Historical Commission erected Marker Number 4131: "On July 17, 1867, three young men were killed in an Indian raid near this site. They were buried in a common grave on John Proffitt's land about one mile south of town. Theirs was the first burial in the community graveyard which became known as Proffitt Cemetery."[113]

# BICKEL-SPANGENBERG, 1868

Not all clashes on the Texas frontier involved Native Americans. However, local tribes were easy scapegoats if thieves or murderers wanted to pin the blame for their crimes on someone else. This seems to have been the case with the Bickel-Spangenberg murders in 1868.

In a report to the *Frontier Times* by Alex Brinkmann, written a day after the murders, he reported the events based on the eyewitness account of the sole

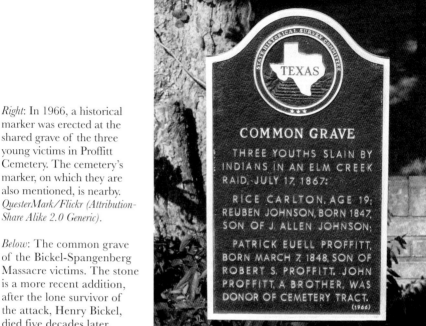

*Right*: In 1966, a historical marker was erected at the shared grave of the three young victims in Proffitt Cemetery. The cemetery's marker, on which they are also mentioned, is nearby. *QuesterMark/Flickr (Attribution-Share Alike 2.0 Generic)*.

*Below*: The common grave of the Bickel-Spangenberg Massacre victims. The stone is a more recent addition, after the lone survivor of the attack, Henry Bickel, died five decades later. *Author's collection*.

survivor. On August 29, John Bickel, a farmer, was drawn out of his home and attacked by robbers. When his neighbor Mr. H. Spangenberg tried to intervene, he was killed, as was John's daughter Catherine Bickel and an unnamed three-year-old Spangenberg child. All had their throats cut. The murderers also stole fifty-five dollars from the Bickel home.

While Brinkmann records that "circumstantial evidence indicates that the assassins were a gang of Mexican horse thieves, who are making our border unsafe,"[114] and the eyewitness also reported the men were Mexican and possibly Anglo, the murderers left evidence attempting to make the killings look like the work of Natives. The gang even made their own arrowheads to leave when they killed cattle or stole horses in order to place the blame on innocent local tribes.

A later report that the men who committed the murders were captured turned out to be incorrect, although as six Mexican men who were connected to the same group of horse thieves were found hanged by vigilantes, this seems to have been considered justice enough, at least for some.

The four victims were buried in a mass grave, the earliest recorded burial in what is now Boerne Cemetery.

John Bickel's son Henry was twelve years old at the time of the attack. He survived by jumping out of a window and fleeing to a nearby farm. He lived until 1917. After his death, he was buried with his family in their shared grave.

## Long Mountain Massacre, 1870

Also known as the Whitlock Family Massacre, after those who were killed, this attack in a normally peaceful area of the state shocked locals in 1870.

The day before the slaughter, a local man who'd had some of his cattle stolen by members of the Comanche tribe lay in wait for a group to pass and took a potshot at them, killing at least one of the group. He got away unharmed after the killing.[115]

The inciting incident had nothing to do with the Whitlock family, farmers originally from South Carolina. They would not have seen the danger they were in, as their murders that same night were retaliation for the murder of the Comanche man.

Soon, smoke was pouring from the Whitlock house. In 1937, a neighbor of the Whitlocks', seventy-eight-year-old Mrs. W.J. Faris, gave an account of the event to *Frontier Times Magazine*. A young girl at the time of the

In 1993, a large marble tombstone was placed on the mass grave of the Whitlock family, quite literally overshadowing the small, worn original. The newer stone reads, in part, "Erected to preserve the history of our valley and honor the founding families who rest here." *Author's collection.*

murders, she claimed to have been close to the doomed family, even visiting with them the Saturday before they were killed. Faris recalled: "Men living nearby saw the fire but reached the Whitlock place too late to save the family. They found the babies that night, and next morning discovered Whitlock's body in the field."[116]

Five members of the Whitlock family, including three children, had been murdered. One young boy was not killed but taken by the Comanches and not seen again (although Faris said she'd "heard he was in Arizona a few years ago.")

The murdered family was buried in a common grave at Hoovers Valley Cemetery in Burnet County, with their funeral paid for by the man who originally attacked the Comanche party.

# BRIT JOHNSON, 1871

In his 1877 work *Historical Sketch of Parker County and Weatherford, Texas,* Henry Smythe wrote a section, "A Most Conspicuous Year Was 1871."

It is true that more clashes between various Native American tribes and colonizers happened apace around that time. Smyth continues, "During the months of that and the previous year, sad and serious consequences resulted to many persons in this vicinity. Murders were frequent, Indian massacres numerous and society in constant agitation. The whole frontier country was kept in a continual state of excitement."[117]

By 1871, Britton Johnson had seen enough hardship to last a lifetime. Born into bondage, it's alleged that he was given some degree of freedom by his enslaver. In 1864, a raiding party of hundreds of Comanches and Kiowas descended on the area, killing Johnson's son and kidnapping his wife and daughters. Johnson searched for them for months, making him a legend, and they were eventually ransomed in 1865.

After the Union victory in the Civil War made him a freedman, Johnson became a teamster. On January 24, 1871, Johnson was in charge of a wagon train and either two or three other teamsters when the men were attacked by about two dozen members of the Kiowa tribe. A second group of teamsters farther off saw the massacre and relayed what happened. While Johnson and all his men were killed, it's said he fought to the last, surrounded by hundreds of shell casings, using the body of his dead horse as a shield.

The teamsters who witnessed the event then buried Johnson and his men in a common grave. The exact location is unknown.

Born in the late 1800s, historian Joseph Carroll McConnell interviewed hundreds of early settlers. In *The West Texas Frontier,* he complied the story of Britt Johnson from interviews with over a dozen people who knew him, including J. B. Terrell, one of the last people to speak to Johnson before he died. From these, McConnell produced a beautiful, if racially tinged, epitaph for the cowboy:

> *Brit and his companions were buried near where they were killed, and on the north side of the old Fort Worth–Fort Belknap military road. And here in an unmarked grave, at the end of his long winding trail, that led to many ranches and cow camps in western Texas, and Indian villages in Oklahoma, lie buried the bones of African Brit Johnson. He was a faithful friend to the whites, was highly esteemed and respected by frontier citizens, and helped write much of the early history of Young and adjoining counties.*[118]

# THE SALT CREEK MASSACRE, 1871

A few months later, in the same area, the Kiowa found themselves in more trouble. They had legitimate grievances: the U.S. government was trying to enforce an unfair treaty that would relocate the tribe to a reservation and severely limit their ability to hunt buffalo. In retaliation, the Kiowa robbed wagon trains, often killing those driving them.

In May 1871, General William Tecumseh Sherman, he of the Civil War's infamous "March to the Sea," was in Texas, and his party was very nearly set upon by a band of Kiowas led by Satanta. Instead, they waited for the next wagon train to pass, at which point the Kiowas attacked.

If the report from the military surgeon who examined the bodies is accurate, the murders were particularly horrible, including one man who was lashed to a wagon wheel and set on fire.[119] In all, seven men were killed. The troops who found the bodies placed all of them in one of the wagons then buried the lot. They marked the grave with stones etched with seven lines.

When confronted, Satanta did not try to hide his participation in the murders, with General Sherman writing, "Satanta again openly admitted the whole affair, and described the attack exactly as the man did to us at Fort Richardson, only denying that any body was tied to the wagon wheel and burned."[120]

*Right*: The marker commemorating the Warren Wagon Train Massacre records that Satanta's death sentence was commuted, but his issues with the Texas legal system would continue until he died in 1878. *Pi3.124/Wikimedia Commons (Creative Commons Attribution-Share Alike 3.0 Unported license).*

*Opposite*: After participating in numerous deadly attacks on wagon trains in 1871, Satanta, a Kiowa war chief (pictured sometime between 1869 and 1874), was arrested and originally sentenced to death. He warned his jury, "If you kill me, it will be a spark on the prairie." C.C. Rister, "SATANTA: Orator of the Plains," *Southwest Review* 17, no. 1, (1932): 77–99. *Library of Congress Prints and Photographs Division.*

Satanta was arrested, tried and sentenced to hang, but the governor of Texas first commuted the sentence to life in prison and then released Satanta on parole. But when he ended up back in prison, Satanta became deeply depressed, stopped eating and eventually died after falling out of a window. While his death is usually considered suicide, his family never accepted this determination.

## Tenth Cavalry Creek, circa 1875

Buffalo Soldier regiments were sent under the command of white officers to the West as muscle to use against hostile Native American tribes. From 1873 to 1875, soldiers from the U.S. Tenth Cavalry served at a fort on Getty's Creek near Burkburnett, Texas, just over the border from Oklahoma. Many of the men were Union veterans of the Civil War and had been stationed at Fort Sill during the conflict.

It's not clear what happened at Tenth Cavalry Creek, what group they were attacked by or even exactly when. By the time a group of cowboys stumbled on the ruins of the fort in the mid-1870s, it was impossible to tell when those stationed there had been killed. The remains of soldiers and horses were strewn across the ground along with debris from the fort. It is believed the dead were buried in a mass grave somewhere in the area, but if this is what happened to their remains, the location has been lost to history.

Because of the lack of information, many sources think the story is a legend. Marker Number 5226, erected near the fort's location in 1970 by the State Historical Survey Committee, acknowledges this. It reads in part, "This staked timber outpost was attacked by Indians; legend says that all the officers, men and horses killed in the battle were buried in a common grave somewhere along this creek."[121]

Sergeant John Harris, pictured in 1871, was a member of the Tenth United States Cavalry Regiment, a Buffalo Soldier unit made up of Black troops. While he did not die at Tenth Cavalry Creek, it would be likely he knew those who did, as he was stationed just across the border at Fort Sill, Oklahoma in 1874. *DeGolyer Library, Southern Methodist University.*

# III

# WAR

Everything about war lends itself to the creation of mass graves. Battles result in hundreds or thousands of deaths. The winning side is often not concerned about showing any special consideration or even basic human decency to the bodies of those who were trying to kill them only a little while before. And after a battle ends, troops often move on quickly, leaving little time for digging numerous individual graves.

In the past two centuries, Texas has seen more than its share of war. Thousands of those who fought in these conflicts ended their days sharing a grave with their comrades.

# 7

# THE MEXICAN WAR OF INDEPENDENCE

I n 1813, so many countries were in open conflict that you could almost call it a world war. But for Americans, this period is often overlooked in school curricula. The War of 1812 is a mystery to most nonhistorians, the only major fact to come out of it and enter popular culture being that the British burned the White House, but not before First Lady Dolley Madison saved a painting of George Washington.

At the time, Britain was warring not just with the United States but also with France's Napoleon Bonaparte, who had taken over most of Western Europe. Meanwhile, Mexico decided this was an ideal time to rebel against Spain. So a group of Anglos and Latinos in present-day Texas tried to take advantage of this confusion with what is termed the "first Texas Revolution."

## THE BATTLE OF MEDINA, 1813

In 1812, a group of antiroyalists who wanted independence for Texas from Spain formed the Gutierrez-Magee Expedition. After a handful of successful skirmishes, they managed to take San Antonio on April 1, 1813. But the decision to execute fifteen Spanish officers split the group, with over one hundred abandoning the cause. It was the beginning of the end.

On August 18, 1813, the remaining members of the Gutierrez-Magee Expedition met Spanish royalist forces at the Battle of Medina. The result was a complete and utter slaughter of the rebels.

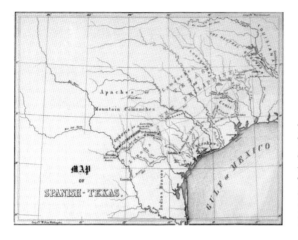

This map of Spanish Texas illustrates the many overlapping societies that wanted their own corner of Texas and were willing to die to defend it. *University of North Texas Libraries, The Portal to Texas History.*

"This was the biggest, bloodiest battle ever fought on Texas soil," Karnes City historian Robert Thonhoff explained to the *Plainview Herald.* "More men were lost at this battle than at the Alamo, Goliad and San Jacinto combined."[122] Estimates range from between 800 and 1,300 dead. Yet, as one former history teacher, who believed he was descended from one of the 90 republican fighters who came out alive, told the same paper, the battle isn't even mentioned in Texas history textbooks.

Texas Historical Commission Marker 13310, located in Leming, notes what happened to the bodies of the fallen long after the guns of the battle went silent: "Eight years later, Mexican leaders ordered the remains of the fallen soldiers to be buried under an oak tree on the battlefield."[123] Left to rot when they died, thrown together in an unmarked mass grave as an afterthought, the insults to the fallen continued, as the location of their burial—and, indeed, of the entire battle itself—has since been lost to history.

Not for lack of trying. There have been many serious attempts to determine the exact coordinates of the conflict, but everyone involved eventually admitted defeat. The closest approximation is that it occurred about twenty miles south of San Antonio. Nine locations are considered feasible, and historical markers erected in three different places each commemorate the battle, but the best they can promise is that it may have happened nearby— meaning the mass grave of the more than one thousand fallen could be there, too.

# 8
# THE TEXAS REVOLUTION

After years of conflict, both political and martial, between the swelling Texian and Tejano population in Texas and the Mexican government, the Texas Revolution officially commenced in 1835. By April, General Santa Anna's forces were defeated at San Jacinto, and the Republic of Texas was born.

However, before that victory, the revolutionaries would see some epic defeats.

## THE BATTLE OF THE ALAMO, 1836

For any Texan, the Battle of the Alamo brings up strong feelings. Many were taught it was the ultimate show of defiance, liberty and comradery. Increasingly, however, historians are reexamining the aims of the colonizers who made their last stand at the Alamo. But what is perhaps most surprising, considering the statewide obsession with the event, is that no one knows what happened to the remains of most of the people who died there.

That is not to say historians have not worked hard to find out. And they've found answers; the problem is that there are too many answers. With so many theories about where the cremated remains of the Alamo defenders were laid to rest, and yet so many questions as well, some in San Antonio decided to come up with their own solution to the riddle, whether it was true or not.

By the end of the thirteen-day siege, which lasted from February 23 to March 6, 1836, almost everyone inside the Alamo mission was dead. While there are no official numbers of casualties or survivors, general estimates are around two hundred and fourteen, respectively. And as there was no one friendly left to bury the dead, it was up to Mexican general Santa Anna and his men to dispose of them.

In a victory dispatch written on March 6, Santa Anna recorded what his men did with the remains of the Alamo defenders: "More than 600 corpses of the foreigners were buried in the ditches and entrenchments."[124] However, this is questionable, since there were certainly not six hundred dead on the Anglo side, and other sources agree that their dead were not buried but burned.

In Mexican colonel José Enrique de la Peña's purported memoir *With Santa Anna in Texas: A Personal Narrative of the Revolution*, he writes of the disposal of the bodies of the Alamo defenders: "within a few hours a funeral pyre rendered into ashes those men who moments before had been so brave that in a blind fury they had unselfishly offered their lives and had met their ends in combat. The greater part of our dead were buried by their comrades, but the enemy, who seems to have some respect for the dead, attributed the great pyre of their dead to our hatred."[125]

A contemporary source backs up this version of events. On March 24, 1836, the *Telegraph and Texas Register* published an account of the battle based on Alamo survivor Susanna Dickinson's information. The paper raged: "Our dead were denied the right of Christian burial; being stripped and thrown into a pile, and burned. Would that we could gather up their ashes and place them in urns!"[126]

Others felt the same. If the Alamo dead were now ash, that ash should at least be respectfully interred.

After defeating Mexico, and almost a year after the fall of the Alamo, Texians returned to honor the remains of their dead. The *Telegraph and Texas Register* published Lieutenant Colonel Juan Seguín's account of the February 25 funeral service in its March 28, 1837 issue. Arriving at the battle site, Seguín and his men found three "heaps" of ashes. They essentially guessed that the two smaller heaps might be the remains of William B. Travis, Davey Crockett and James Bowie, while the larger ones must have been everyone else. After gathering the heaps of ash into three coffins, Seguín writes: "The procession then proceeded to the principal spot and places of internment, where the graves had been prepared.…The coffin and all the ashes were then interred, and three volleys of musquetry [*sic*] were fired by the whole battalion."[127]

This would seemingly be the definitive answer to what was done with the Alamo defenders' remains, but Seguín himself complicated things fifty-two years later. When the former Speaker of the Texas House of Representatives Hamilton P. Bee wrote to Seguín in 1889 in a desperate attempt to learn the exact location Seguín and his men had buried the coffins, he was given a completely different story. Seguín wrote: "The remains of those who died at the Alamo were ordered burned by Gen. Santana, and the few fractions I ordered deposited in an urn. I ordered a sepulture opened in the Cathedral of San Antonio immediately at the presbytery; that is, in front of the railing, but very near the steps. This is all I can tell you concerning this matter."[128]

However, the cathedral denied this version of events and has no records of it happening. Politician and judge José María Rodríguez was a child when he saw the Battle of the Alamo from a distance, and he agrees that Seguín got his facts confused in his later recollection.

> *There has been a great deal of discussion with reference to what had been done with the bodies of the Texans who were slain in the Alamo. It is claimed that Col. Seguin wrote a letter in which he stated that he got together the ashes in the following February and put them in an iron urn and buried them in San Fernando Cathedral. This does not seem possible to me, because nothing of that kind could have happened without us knowing that and we never heard of any occurrence of that kind....It is true that the bones were brought together somewhere in the neighborhood or little east of where the Menninger Hotel is now and were buried by Col. Seguin, but that any of them were ever buried in the Cathedral, I have never heard nor do I believe that to be true.[129]*

After intense research, in 1999, the Center for Archaeological Research at the University of Texas at San Antonio produced the report "Historical and Archaeological Investigations at the Site of Rivercenter Mall (Las Tiendas)," which included a chapter titled "Searching for the Funeral Pyre." The researchers did not find the location, but they did unequivocally rule one out, stating, "the only place that can safely be eliminated from contention is beneath the Cenotaph," even though the impressive monument is, perhaps logically, "the place most tourists assume is the site of their burial."[130]

So, there is little question the bodies of the Alamo dead were burned and that some of the resulting ashes were later interred. The most likely location? A peach orchard.

The Englishman William Bollaert was traveling through Texas at the time of the funeral and later wrote that the burial took place in a "peach orchard" near the Alamo. Dr. John Sutherland was in San Antonio and would have almost certainly died at the Alamo had he not been badly injured when his horse fell on him, making him useless to those in the mission. He later wrote that the men's remains were buried in "a peach orchard, not far from the scene of the last charge and struggle." Historian Reuben M. Potter, who around 1861 went to San Antonio and interviewed Seguín in his attempts to locate the grave, determined that "the place of burial was a peach orchard then outside of the Alamo Village and a few hundred yards from the Fort."[131]

Unfortunately, no one knows where this peach orchard was located. In 1868, in his article "The Fall of the Alamo," Potter lamented that the location of the grave "is now densely built over, and its identity is irrevocably lost. This is too sad for comment."[132] Ten years later, Potter further explained that by the time he went looking for the grave a quarter century after the battle, "the rude landmarks which had once pointed out the place of sepulture had long since disappeared."[133]

In 1906, Charles Merritt Barnes, writing in the *San Antonio Daily Express*, relayed the Battle of the Alamo eyewitness Pablo Diaz's recollections. Diaz said he saw the funeral pyre burning for two full days. His recollections were corroborated by a second source of Barnes's, who had a bit more information to share.

> [Antonio] *Perez goes further than Diaz and says that for many years there was a small mound there under which he was told the charred bones that the fire did not consume were buried by some humane persons who had to do so secretly, and he was familiar with the spot as the burial place of Bowie and Crockett. Perez states that about 30 years ago these bones were exhumed and placed in the old city Cemetery....But he does not know the part of that cemetery they were placed in.*[134]

Allegedly, someone else did know. While it is based on the most tenuous of evidence, the Alamo Defenders Descendants Association placed a marker in an unassuming, easy-to-miss location in San Antonio's Oddfellows Cemetery in 2004. It states:

> *August Beisenbach, city clerk of San Antonio states that when he was an 8 year old boy playing on the Alameda (Commerce St.) he witnessed*

The grave holding the remains of the Alamo defenders is said to be to the right of this monument to Captain Robert Addison Gillespie, for whom Gillespie County is named. If true, the remains would have been interred a decade after the Texas Ranger was laid to rest. *Author's collection.*

> *the exhuming of bodies or remains consisting of bones and fragments of bones, of victims of the siege of The Alamo that had been interred near the place where the bodies had been burned and originally buried, and saw their transfers from that place to the old cemetery, on Powder House Hill (Oddfellows Cemetery) this, he states, happened in 1856. The fragments of the bodies had been first buried in 1836 and some in 1837. Mr. Beisenbach states that these bodies are buried midway between the monuments of Capt. R.A. Gillespe and Capt. Samuel H. Walker.[135]*

While this guess may be as good as any, the location is not accepted by local or state historical societies, which is why there is no more official marker. In his seminal work of Texas history, *Lone Star*, T.R. Fehrenbach stated plainly: "The charred remains of the Alamo dead were dumped in a common grave. Its location went unrecorded and was never found."[136]

## THE BATTLE OF REFUGIO, 1836

The Battle of Refugio took place from March 12 to 15, 1836, only a week after the Battle of the Alamo's culmination. Captain Amon B. King and Lieutenant Colonel William Ward were supposed to be evacuating the Anglo population of the Refugio Mission. Instead, King disobeyed a direct order, and the two leaders found themselves and their approximately 150 men engaged in combat with a Mexican force of 1,500 under the command of General José de Urrea.

After a confused, messy fight, hundreds of Mexican soldiers were dead, although the exact number is unknown. Despite their losses, the Mexican forces saw the battle as a victory, as they captured or scattered the Texian troops and ultimately took Refugio Mission. Colonist Sabina Brown Fox was living there with her family and later recalled what happened next: "After they had robbed us of everything of value they commanded to pile up their dead, which made a pile as big as twenty cords of wood. Poland had fenced in his town lot with a ditch four feet deep and four feet wide, they began to drag their dead into it and throw them in and filled it to the top then they raked the dirt in on it and this caused his lot to be marked with a ridge."[137]

Texas Historical Commission Marker Number 5934, located at the site of the old mission, repeats this story almost to the word.[138]

While Ward and his men managed to retreat (at least temporarily), King and most of his men were captured by the Mexican forces and executed. A monument to the soldiers was erected in Refugio in 1936. It is adorned by Marker Number 152, which states:

> *On March 16, 1836, Captain King and fourteen of his men who had been made prisoners by General Urrea's cavalry the day before were marched to the slope of the hill on Goliad Road about one mile from the Refugio church and shot. Their bones were later buried where they fell by John Hynes, a twelve year old lad of Refugio who had been their friend. James Murphy of Refugio Colonel Fannin's courier killed nearby on March 14, was buried in their common grave.*[139]

## THE BATTLE OF COLETO (GOLIAD), 1836

"When you ask people what they think about the Alamo, they tell you immediately what comes to mind: never give up; fight to the death; an absolute right and wrong," author John Willingham told the *San Antonio Express-News* in 2011. "Goliad is more complex."[140]

While the Alamo has gone down in history and is world-famous, the battle that took place only two weeks later never made it into the public consciousness. And it seems this amnesia was something that happened almost immediately afterward. In 1939, the Honorable Harbert Davenport bemoaned that "though part of the Texan battle cry at San Jacinto was 'Remember Goliad!'…'Remember the Alamo!' was what the Texans really meant. 'Forget Goliad!' would have been a more correct expression of the mingled shame and pride with which early Texans regarded Fannin's men."

After the disastrous loss at the Battle of Refugio, Lieutenant Colonel William Ward reunited his remaining forces with Colonel James W. Fannin in Goliad. On March 19, 1836, the whole company retreated on the orders of General Sam Houston, who wanted to regroup his forces in Victoria. But Fannin and his men would not make it. Near Coleto Creek, General José de Urrea caught up with them. After attempting to hold out and repelling three attacks, Fannin surrendered on the morning of March 20.

Now prisoners of war, the Texians were marched back to Presidio La Bahía in Goliad. While survivors would later say they were promised safety when they surrendered, General Santa Anna demanded they be executed, based on the Tornel Decree. Passed in December 1835, the decree stated that all armed foreigners "with the object of attacking our territory, shall be treated and punished as pirates."[141] In plain terms, this meant there would be no quarter for prisoners of war; they would be killed. Santa Anna demanded this decree be carried out against the men at Goliad. However, Urrea refused, and it was left to Lieutenant Colonel José Nicolás de la Portilla to do the deed.

On March 27, Palm Sunday, exactly three weeks after the fall of the Alamo, over four hundred Texian prisoners were escorted from the Presidio. One of them, Sergeant Isaac D. Hamilton, was badly wounded but ultimately survived the massacre. He was therefore one of the few Texians who could give an eyewitness account of what occurred. In a sworn statement given in 1852, Hamilton said that Fannin's men surrendered to Urrea only "under the stipulations that we should be treated as prisoners of war and returned to the United States in safety both in person and property." Consequently, it was a shock to all of them when "we were marched back to Goliad where on the sixth day, after the battle, before sunrise we were marched some hundred yards from the fort when the first intimation we received that the articles of the treaty would not be complied

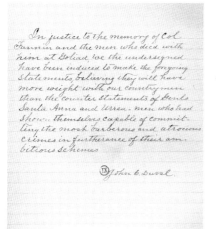

Feeling that Santa Anna's version of the events at Goliad was inaccurate, survivor John C. Duval wrote a statement telling the Texian side of the story. The final page of the document reads: "In justice to the memory of Col Fannin and the men who died with him at Goliad, we the undersigned have been induced to make the foregoing statements, believing they will have more weight with our countrymen than the counter statements of Genls Santa Anna and Urrea—men who had shown themselves capable of committing the most barbarous and atrocious crimes in furtherance of their ambitious schemes." *Texas State Library and Archives.*

with was an order—now in Spanish—for us to be shot. The question being asked if any one of us could speak Spanish and answered in the negative the order to face about was given in English. This order some obeyed while others refused. The order to fire was then given."[142]

Those who did not die after being shot were bayonetted or beaten to death. At least 400 men, possibly as many as 450, were killed. Only 28 survived, most by pretending to be dead. Lieutenant Colonel William Ward, who had narrowly escaped Captain Amon B. King's fate at the Battle of Refugio two weeks before, was one of those executed. General Fannin was the last man killed. The bodies were dumped in trenches or burned.

It was not until the defeat of Santa Anna at the Battle of San Jacinto on April 21 that any soldiers could be spared to return for the remains of the Goliad Massacre victims. General Thomas J. Rusk entered Goliad on June 3 and found the uncovered, partially burned bodies being eaten by coyotes and wild dogs. He immediately ordered a military funeral with full honors.

The next day, in the presence of some of the men who had survived the massacre, Rusk spoke over the newly dug common grave during the funeral. He said, "In that mass of remains and fragments of bones, many a mother might see her son, many a sister her brother, and many a wife her own beloved and affectionate husband."[143]

Texans promptly forgot about the grave site. Very few remembered the location, marked only by a small pile of stones placed by a local man in the 1850s. And it might have remained forgotten had the mass grave not been rediscovered accidentally in 1930 by a Boy Scout troop when its members found bits of bone around the rock pile.

The imposing monument to the casualties of Goliad was designed by Donald Nelson and constructed of Marble Falls pink granite in 1939. The foundation of the Fannin Memorial Monument is circular and surrounds the mass grave of Colonel James Fannin and his men. The dramatic bas-relief represents "Texas honoring her heroes." Commission of Control for Texas Centennial Celebrations. Monuments Erected By The State Of Texas To Commemorate The Centenary Of Texas Independence: The Report Of The Commission Of Control For Texas Centennial Celebrations, Austin: The Steck Company, 1938. *P6150/ Wikimedia Commons (Creative Commons Attribution-Share Alike 3.0 Unported license).*

As part of the memorial-building frenzy that surrounded Texas's centennial in 1936, a grand monument was planned for the four hundred men who had been forgotten for so long.

Speaking at the dedication of the Fannin Memorial Monument in 1939, the Honorable Harbert Davenport opined:

> *It is not to the credit of Texas that the men of Goliad should have reposed for a century in an unmarked, un-honored, and almost unknown grave. A hundred and three years have passed since the Texan Army, having retaken Goliad, buried their bones where they now lie; and since Gen. Rusk, betrayed by his feelings, broke down in attempting to deliver the simple though eloquent eulogy he had prepared for delivery at their grave. Even now, when Texas, at a very long last, has remembered them, their monument is not in keeping with some that have them builded, to commemorate smaller men and less important deeds. But their real memorials are elsewhere; this one but preserves their names and marks their grave.*[144]

# THE DAWSON MASSACRE, 1842

Texas won its independence in 1836, but the Mexican government did not give up so easily. It continued launching attacks on the Republic of Texas for many years.

On September 11, 1842, Mexican brigadier general Adrián Woll and his 1,600-strong force made it all the way to San Antonio, capturing the city with little resistance. The Texians could not allow this and quickly raised two militias, which headed toward San Antonio.

Nicholas Mosby Dawson led the smaller of these retaliatory forces, with just fifty-three volunteers. Nearing the city, the group found itself facing five hundred Mexican cavalry and two cannons. As his men fell around him, Dawson knew his only choice was to surrender. But when he raised the white flag, neither side stopped fighting. Barely an hour after engaging the enemy, thirty-six of the fifty-four Texians were dead, including Dawson.

Two days later, Mathew Caldwell, the leader of the second Texian militia, had managed to drive General Woll's forces from San Antonio. Caldwell and his men buried the casualties of the Dawson Expedition in shallow graves where they had fallen. But the mesquite thicket where they lay would not be their final resting place.

# THE BLACK BEAN DEATH LOTTERY, 1843

The Dawson Massacre incensed the citizens of Texas. A volunteer force under the command of General Alexander Somervell swelled to 750 men, all of whom wanted revenge. Finally on the move, in Laredo the group became a mob, raping and pillaging. Many abandoned the expedition in disgust at the actions of their fellow militants. Somervell had lost control of his troops.[145]

The disorder in the ranks made it easier for Mexican forces under General Pedro de Ampudia when the two sides clashed on Christmas Day 1842. After almost twenty-four hours of vicious combat, more than two hundred Texians surrendered.

The next few months included a forced march toward Mexico City, a mass-escape attempt by almost all the Texian prisoners and a desperate run north to the border. However, 176 of the prisoners were recaptured and taken to Salado. Furious at both the escape and the expedition's heinous crimes in Laredo, President Santa Anna demanded all the men be killed.

Frederic Remington's oil on canvas *The Mier Expedition: The Drawing of the Black Bean*, painted in 1896, is now in the collection of the Museum of Fine Arts, Houston. *The Hogg Brothers Collection, gift of Miss Ima Hogg.*

When his underlings balked at the order, it was decided the Texian ranks would be decimated.

In order to decide which 17 of the 176 men would be executed, the Mexican officers informed the Texians they would be selecting beans from a jar. If a man pulled a white bean, he would live. Those who found a black bean in their palm would be shot.

William A.A. "Big Foot" Wallace survived the Meir Expedition and later wrote a haunting account of the Black Bean Lottery.

> *Those who drew black beans seemed to care very little about it. Occasionally one would remark, as he drew out the fatal color, "Well, boys, the jig is up with me;" or, "They have taken my sign in at last;" or something of a similar character, and then give way to the next, apparently as unconcerned as if he had no interest whatever in what was going on around him.*
>
> *There was but a single exception to this. One poor fellow, a messmate of mine, too, appeared to be completely overcome by his apprehensions of drawing a black bean. He stood until his own time to draw came round, wringing his hands and moaning audibly, and continually telling those near him that he knew he should draw a black bean; that he had a presentiment*

The forty-eight-foot-tall memorial to the victims of the Dawson Massacre and the Black Bean Death Lottery was erected in 1936–37. The colorful Art Deco mural depicts the latter episode. Sculptor Raoul Josset, who also worked on the Goliad Massacre monument, created the ten-foot bronze angel statue at the base. *Larry D. Moore, CC BY-SA 3.0, Wikimedia Commons.*

*such would be his fate. When his turn came, he hung back, and absolutely refused to go up at all until a file of Mexican soldiers forced him forward at the points of their bayonets. He hesitated so long after he put his hand into the vessel containing the beans that a Mexican officer near him pricked him severely with his sword to make him withdraw it.…At last the poor fellow was forced to withdraw his hand, and his presentiment proved too true, for in it he held the fatal black bean. He turned deadly pale as his eyes rested upon it, but apparently he soon resigned himself to his inevitable fate, for he never uttered a word of complaint afterward. I pitied him from the bottom of my heart.*[146]

The unlucky seventeen were taken out and shot and their bodies buried in Mexico.

In 1848, the remains of the Meir Expedition casualties were repatriated to Texas, and those of the Dawson Massacre victims were disinterred from San Antonio. Both groups were brought to La Grange for burial.

Franciska Vogt was thirteen at the time. On her ninety-third birthday in 1928, she gave an interview to the *La Grange Journal* about the event eighty years before. "Ah, I shall never forget how it looked," she said, "that procession of men riding mules and leading others with the bones of the Texans slung in gunny-sacks across the backs of the animals. They came right into town, and when I heard what was going to be done, I remember I ran and jumped on my pony and raced to the top of the hill for the ceremony." Understandably, the memory of the day was not crystal clear after eight decades. Vogt admitted, "I do not remember much of what happened, except that it was all very solemn and quiet as the bones were carefully and tenderly buried up there on the hill. Then the monument was put up—the big limestone tomb under which are the remains of those seventeen men who drew the black beans of death."[147]

In fact, it was the remains of fifty-two men in all that were laid to rest in this common grave. Two coffins hold the remains, one for the victims of each of the ill-fated expeditions. Texas Historical Commission Marker Number 12756 records simply: "In September 1848, the remains of Texans killed in the 1842 Dawson Massacre and the 1843 'Black Bean Death Lottery' were reburied at this site in a sandstone vault."[148]

In 1937, an elaborate, forty-eight-foot-tall Art Deco monument was erected above the mass grave.

# 9

# THE MEXICAN-AMERICAN WAR

Most history classes don't spend too much time on the Mexican-American War. Americans in the 1840s would find this astonishing to the point of disbelief. In 2007, the director of the Palo Alto Battlefield National Historical Park, Douglas Murphy, told *Texas Parks and Wildlife* magazine: "In the newspapers at the time, the opening battles were presented as one of the biggest events of American history. It was the equivalent of Bunker Hill and it would never be forgotten."[149]

It's clear why they thought so. The United States annexed Texas in 1845, but the border between Texas and Mexico had never been agreed on. One year later, President James K. Polk sent troops to the state and the Mexican government sent its own troops. Violence was inevitable. The war lasted eighteen months and was a complete and total victory for the United States. In the end, the Rio Grande became the border between the two countries.

But the war that resulted in the definitive southern border of the United States and added millions of acres of land to the southwest portion of the country, the war that thrust the general in charge into the White House, is today little more than a historical footnote for the average American.

## Resaca de la Palma, 1846

The Battle of Resaca de la Palma was technically just a continuation of the Battle of Palo Alto, which had taken place the day before, on May 8, 1846.

A lithograph of the Battle of Resaca de la Palma published in 1846 shows General (later President) Zachary Taylor giving orders to Captain Charles May. Bodies litter the battlefield around them. *Library of Congress.*

And both battles occurred before the United States formally declared war on Mexico on May 13.

It was a vicious clash, with hand-to-hand combat between the two sides. The U.S. forces captured the Mexican artillery, forcing the Mexicans to retreat. Further misfortune befell the Mexican soldiers as they fled, including many who drowned trying to get back across the Rio Grande.

The decisive victory allowed General Zachary Taylor and his troops to cross into Mexico, where the majority of the rest of the war would take place.

Taylor's official report on the Battle of Resaca de la Palma stated that his troops buried 200 Mexican soldiers the day after the conflict. Other government documents list a total of 262. However, Mexican records indicate they lost only 160 men in the battle. Regardless, the number was in the hundreds, and the field was strewn with bodies.

Author Thomas Bangs Thorpe was not part of the fight but was, in his own words, "on the battlefields, and among the heroes, almost immediately after the occurrences" which he wrote about in his book *Our Army on the Rio Grande.* He was witness to the carnage and the disposition of the remains of the fallen.

*The last sepulchral rites having been performed for our own countrymen, humanity dictated the same respect to the fallen foe. Many of the wounded, and all of the dead of the Mexican army, had been left upon the field; and as the sun rose high in the heavens, and poured its scorching rays upon these mouldering masses, the scent of blood filled the air. The buzzard, high above, wheeled in lessening circles over its prospective feast, while the foul jackals, that had made the night hideous with their moans, were seen surlily skulking from the eyes of our soldiery, who were busy in gathering together the Mexican dead for burial in one common grave.* [150]

Some of the more important American casualties of the battle were buried where they fell before their bodies were later disinterred and returned to their families. An article in the *York Republican* on December 23, 1846, detailed what one such journey entailed, when doctors traveled to Resaca de la Palma to recover the remains of Lieutenant Richard E. Cochran. Their reverence for the deceased evidently did not extend to the remains of those on the other side of the conflict, as the author of the article told readers, "Immediately on our arrival, we dispatched a man to the Palo Alto battlefield to procure us some Mexican skulls—a few of which we have with us." [151]

In 1848, Helen Chapman, one of the first residents of Brownsville—only a few miles from the battlefield—took a day trip to see the infamous place. She wrote, "We came to a very beautiful spot, a large green open space which was the camping ground of General José Arista where all his baggage and booty was found. On the opposite side of the road are two large circular places where the turf has been turned up, and there lie the bodies of those who fell upon the field. Two large pits were dug and into were thrown Americans and Mexicans." [152]

An accidental discovery of one of these mass graves in 1967 proved that the contemporary accounts were accurate. During the construction of a housing subdivision in Brownsville, multiple skeletal remains were uncovered. Three graduate students from the University of Texas at Austin excavated the grave. (It is believed there were more graves uncovered during construction, but as the excavation delayed the building activities, they were simply not mentioned to the students.) Decades later, in 2015, one of the graduate students from the earlier excavation, Thomas R. Hester, wrote a paper, published in the *Bulletin of the Texas Archeological and Paleontological Society*. He explained, "It was immediately clear that there were multiple individuals, many overlapping, or lying atop or under

BURYING THE DEAD AFTER THE BATTLE OF MONTEREY

Four months after the Battle of Resaca de la Palma, Mexican and U.S. forces met in Monterey, Mexico. This painting of the grisly aftermath shows troops burying their dead on the battlefield. *University of Texas at Arlington Library, Special Collections.*

other remains. And, as we expose the remains, it was also obvious that partial skeletons represented some individuals. As these observations were confirmed, we realize that the victims from the battle had been dropped or thrown into a large grave pit."[153]

# 10

# THE CIVIL WAR

The Civil War did not bring out the best in some Texans. For a certain type of Confederate, it was not enough that their neighbors passively accept their new country but actively support it. And any hint of Union sympathy could be deadly.

## Dead Man's Hole, Marble Falls, circa 1861

Near Marble Falls, Ferdinand Lueders made a fascinating discovery in 1821. While looking for bugs, the entomologist stumbled upon a deep cave. Belched out of the earth's crust by pressure from subterranean gas, the cave was found to be over 160 feet deep when it was finally fully explored in the 1950s and '60s. Yet the entrance to the cave is comparatively tiny, only 7 feet in diameter. While this cave could have been nothing more than a fascinating geological feature for the people of Marble Falls to enjoy, during the Civil War, the hole became an entrance to hell itself.

Burnett County did not vote to secede from the Union but had little choice once Texas did. Perhaps because they were outnumbered in their area, pro-Confederate men formed vigilante groups that hunted down those who held different views. Many Union sympathizers found themselves at the end of a rope hung from an oak tree above Dead Man's Hole before they were cut down and their bodies fell into the cave. So many were hanged there that it is said the tree branch had marks from the ropes cut into it.

Dead Man's Hole near Marble Falls is still ominous, even with the long drop blocked off by a metal sheet. It is easy to imagine the terror felt by the men who were marched to the tree and stared into their dark grave before being hanged. *Author's collection.*

Texas Historical Commission Marker Number 11772 notes that up to seventeen corpses may have called Dead Man's Hole their final resting place, "including those of pro-Union Judge John R. Scott and settler Adolph Hoppe, several reconstruction-era county government officials, and Ben McKeever, who had a conflict with local freedmen."[154] Other sources say the number might be more than thirty.

Various oral histories give different details on when and how men thrown in the hole were killed. But what is definite is that the hole became a dumping ground for those who supported the Union, both during and after the Civil War. Despite the danger from the toxic gas that lingered within the cave, some families managed to recover the remains of their loved ones from Dead Man's Hole. Other bodies were left down there, with the cave becoming their mass grave.

The cave's marker was erected in 1998, and one year later, land around it was donated to Burnet County as a park. To ensure modern visitors do not accidentally join the Unionists in the cave's mass grave, the opening to the dark hole is now blocked by a metal sheet.

## Dᴇᴀᴅ Mᴇɴ's Hᴏʟᴇ, Gɪʟʟᴇsᴘɪᴇ Cᴏᴜɴᴛʏ, 1862

Around the same time, more unlucky Texans found themselves in a completely different grave, known locally as "Dead Men's Hole." While less well known, Spring Creek Cemetery in Harper hosts the common grave of four men: Sebird Henderson, Hiram Nelson, Charles "Frank" Scott and Gus Tegener. Like those in the Marble Falls "Dead Man's Hole," these men found themselves on the "wrong" side of the Civil War. In July 1862, the Union supporters were arrested by Captain James Duff, who was in charge of making local men swear allegiance to the Confederacy on pain of death. These four men would not and, for their beliefs, were hanged. Then their bodies were thrown into a nearby creek.

In a 2009 interview, Wanda Henderson told the *West Kerr Current* how the men came to lie together in the Spring Creek Cemetery: "Their widows, and their children, were taken as prisoners to Fort Martin Scott. Later, the soldiers brought the women and children down to the creek, where they took the husbands' bodies out. They dug one big common grave, put their husbands on sheets, and buried them." She added, "We don't think about those atrocities anymore these days—it's been so long ago."

A metal wreath that had been used to mark the grave was unearthed in 1982, and a tombstone was added. Along with their names and years of death, the stone records how they died…and the man who killed them.

## THE NUECES MASSACRE, 1862

As the Confederate military began to impress able-bodied men into service, those who did not believe in the Southern cause or did not want to fight at all became desperate. Most German immigrants to Central Texas had no intention of joining the conflict. And some not only did not support the Confederacy but also wanted to fight for the Union.

Such was the decision a group of about sixty-three young German men (plus five Anglos and one Mexican) came to in August 1862. While attempting to make it to Mexico, and from there to New Orleans to join the Union forces, they were attacked by ninety-four Confederate troops led by Lieutenant C.D. McRae on August 10 on the Nueces River near Comfort.

Knowing they were sitting ducks and carrying too few arms, the German militia's commander yelled, "Lasst uns unser Leben so teuer wie möglich verkaufen" ("Let us sell our lives as dear as we can").[155]

Nineteen of them died in the fighting that followed. A few months later, six of the men who had escaped and continued to Mexico were killed once they reached the Rio Grande.

Nine badly wounded Germans were taken prisoner by the Confederates. These men also died, but not in battle.

In his memoir, Captain Robert Hamilton Williams of the Texas Rangers recalled the shameful and immoral murder of the immigrants. The injured were bound and led away to a more secluded area, ostensibly to get them out of the punishing sun. Then, Williams writes, "The sound of firing was heard a little way off. I thought at first they were burying some of the dead with the honours of war; but it didn't sound like that either."

It took a minute for the reality of what just happened to sink in. Williams's account continues: "'It can't possibly be they have murdered the prisoners in cold blood!' I said, not believing that even Luck [Lieutenant Edwin Lilly] would be guilty of such an atrocious crime. 'Oh yes; they're all dead, sure enough—and a good job too!' Feeling sick at heart, though I hardly even then credited his report, I ran on, and found it only too true."

FUNERAL OF GERMAN PATRIOTS AT COMFORT, TEXAS, August 20, 1865.—[See Page 89.]

The January 20, 1866 edition of *Harper's Weekly* ran an image of the "Funeral of German patriots at Comfort, Texas, August 20, 1865" on its front cover. *Library of Congress.*

After this coldhearted slaughter, it is unsurprising the Confederate soldiers did not give the men they had murdered a proper burial. Williams wrote, "Our own dead were buried in one long trench, but those of the enemy were carried to where the murdered prisoners lay, and there left for a prey to the buzzards and coyotes."[156]

These deaths were arguably war crimes. The event became known as the Nueces Massacre.

The bodies of the Union supporters lied there until the end of the war. Finally, on August 13, 1865, Major General Canby sent instructions to Brigadier General J.R. West: "The Major General Commanding directs that you detach from your command one hundred men properly officered to proceed to Comfort and there establish a camp....The remains of some Union men who were killed by the Rebels in 1863 [*sic*] are to be buried at Comfort on the 17th inst. And the general desires that the Military at Comfort turn out on the occasion."[157]

Captain John W. Sansom was a survivor of the battle and later wrote his own account of the event. He explained what happened to the bodies of his compatriots, although he underestimated the number killed: "Nineteen in all, not one of whom was buried by the slayers; but three years later, in 1865, all the bones to be found of those nineteen martyrs to their

*Left*: A stereograph of the Treue der Union Monument. The photo was taken shortly after the installation of the obelisk in 1866. *DeGolyer Library, Southern Methodist University.*

*Below*: A modern view of the Treue der Union Monument in Comfort, Texas. *Author's collection.*

convictions were gathered together by their relatives and friends, and buried…with all the solemnity due to the last remains of good citizens and true patriots."[158]

The funeral took place on August 20, 1865. It was attended by an estimated three hundred mourners. A marker at the site records that E. Degener, who had lost two sons in the massacre, gave a moving eulogy, which ended on this poignant note: "The sacrifice that we, the fathers of the slaughtered, made to our country and to liberty, is great and dolorous. We shall, however, console ourselves; we shall be proud of having offered our sons to the Union. If the glorious victory of its arms bear all the fruits that the nation and the whole of humanity justly expect to reap."[159]

The mass grave of the Unionists at Comfort would become more elaborate as time went on. A year after the funeral, a twenty-foot-tall limestone obelisk was erected at the site. Three historical markers were added over the years by the State Historical Survey Committee and the Comfort Heritage Foundation. The Treue der Union (Loyalty to the Union) Monument was restored in 1994, and a thirty-six-star American flag still flies at half-mast at the grave site.

## THE GREAT HANGING AT GAINESVILLE, 1862

While the murders of Unionists in Texas during the Civil War were horrific, the Great Hanging at Gainesville is notable even among those atrocities. Forty men in and around Gainesville were murdered in the span of a week. Most were hanged, usually in groups. Some were shot. None had committed a crime, and none received due process.

Texas Historical Commission Marker Number 5347 is a good reminder that history can quite literally be rewritten. Erected in 1964, coming up to the centenary of the South's loss and at the height of the civil rights movement, it is clearly concerned more with modern politics than any accurate version of history. It is so egregious an example of this problem that it was covered at length in bestselling author James W. Loewen's *Lies Across America: What Our Historic Sites Get Wrong*. The marker's claims about possible invasions and its attempts to make it seem as if the victims got their day in court are not backed up by contemporary sources.

In truth, these victims were effectively lynched for not appearing pro-Confederacy enough to the enslavers of the area. Worked into a frenzy over imaginary dangers, mobs strung up innocent man after innocent man.

The February 20, 1864 edition of *Frank Leslie's Illustrated Newspaper* dedicated the centerfold spread to "Rebel Barbarities in Texas." The central image depicted the "Hanging of 30 Union Men" at Gainesville. *Frank Leslie's Illustrated Newspaper/Wikimedia Commons.*

The hangings at Gainesville were trumpeted in the North as proof of Southern—specifically Texan—barbarity. While the governor and other state authorities condoned the actions, the president of the Confederacy, Jefferson Davis, was not happy about the murders.

## THE HANGING TREE, 1863

Another group of eight men who did not want to fight for the Confederacy left Williamson County in 1863, heading for Mexico. They made no secret of where or why they were going. When they were accosted by a group of cavalrymen led by Major William J. Alexander, they agreed to return peacefully in exchange for fair trials.

As they were marched back toward Bandera, however, some of the soldiers decided to kill the prisoners right then. That night, each man was hanged one by one in a slow, agonizing manner. One of the men, knowing there was no way out and preferring to die in a less painful way, asked to be shot. A soldier responded by using "a full charge, the ramrod being left in the gun and penetrated though [the prisoner's] body." The corpses were left on the ground, each with a noose still around its neck, but not before the soldiers emptied their pockets of money and other valuables.

Local men found the bodies the next day and were horrified, originally believing it was the work of Native Americans.

In 1922, when he was eighty-six years old, George Hay, one of the men who found the bodies, recalled the slaughter: "I have seen many foul crimes in my time, but this was the most revolting that I ever knew. A party of us went out from Bandera as soon as we learned of the occurrence and found the bodies of those unfortunate men lying just as they had them cut down, pieces of the horse-hair rope around each man's neck."[160]

The locals buried the men. In the same interview, John Pyke said he was "just a lad, large enough however, to think I was about grown," at the time of the hanging. "We dug a shallow grave, laid the dead men into it, spread blankets over them, and covered them up the best we could with dirt and stones to keep the wolves from getting to the bodies."[161]

The August 1924 edition of J. Marvin Hunter's *Frontier Times Magazine* recorded, "A grave was opened, and the bodies were rolled into it and covered up. Many years later, a tombstone was erected over the grave, and on this tombstone appear the names of the men who were murdered while prisoners, who had been given a sacred pledge that they would be given just treatment if they surrendered."[162] The grave is on private property near Bandara.

The men who committed the murders were never punished.

# DOVE CREEK, 1865

While technically a Civil War battle, the fighting at Dove Creek was anything but typical for that conflict. On January 8, 1865, in the middle of a snowstorm, Confederate troops stalked and then attacked unprovoked a migrating group of Kickapoos on Dove Creek in present-day Tom Green County. While various Confederate survivors would report they were vastly outnumbered by their foe, the Kickapoo group also included many women and children, as it was simply traveling to a new camp.

The Kickapoo were already in a well-protected, almost impenetrable location, and the two Confederate units, led by men who did not like one another, had no cohesion. The decision to attack the tribe seems absurd.

It was, unsurprisingly, a disaster for the Confederate soldiers. They lost three officers and sixteen enlisted men almost as soon as the attack began. While historians are uncertain what the final casualties came to, it was at least twenty-two dead and nineteen wounded, as well as the deaths of dozens of the cavalry's horses. Many soldiers went AWOL during and after the battle. The next day, stuck in the snow, wet and freezing, some of the Confederate survivors were forced to kill and eat their horses.

Accounts vary on who returned to bury the bodies of the dead soldiers and when, but by March 1865, a group of men deposited the remains in a single grave on the battlefield.

A cenotaph erected in 1936 by the state of Texas reads, "Around this mountain a battle was fought between 2,000 Indians and Texas Rangers and state troops commanded by Captains John Fossett and S.S. Totten. Four officers and 22 other men lie in unmarked graves nearby."[163]

# IV

# EXTRAJUDICIAL KILLINGS, LYNCHINGS AND MURDERS

There is no acceptable number of murders; even one is too many. But when a person or persons commit enough murders all at once to fill a mass grave? That is another level of overkill.

# 11

# KENTUCKYTOWN HANGING, 1864

L ife in rural Texas during the 1800s was a mix of willingness to help friends and strangers who came to your door at any time, day or night, and the possibility those visitors might have something far less neighborly on their minds.

In 1864, the Stevenson family of Kentuckytown was settling down for the night when a group of men (different sources say three or six, one of many details they do not agree on) called for Mr. Stevenson to join them outside. When he did, they demanded his gold.

Stevenson had returned from the California Gold Rush in possession of a large fortune, which he was not shy about spending. The robbers appeared to believe the only logical place for him to keep his wealth was buried on his farm somewhere.

Determined to torture him into giving up the location of the gold, the men hanged Stevenson almost to death, twice, from a tree in front of his wife (possibly named Polly) and their children. They also threatened to rape Polly. When hanging Stevenson a third time, they fled, possibly due to a shooting star they interpreted as a bad sign. It's not clear if they left with any gold, although the contemporary account in Austin's *Weekly State Gazette* reports they did get away with a "large amount of money."[164] Polly was able to revive her husband, barely, but news about the attempted murder and would-be robbers spread around a nervous county.

Two of the men were quickly arrested, which led to five other men being taken into custody. The law was in every position to do its job, but this was not good enough for a posse of "150 well-armed men" from the local area. While the prisoners were being transferred to Bonham for their trial, the posse demanded the sheriff turn the men over to them.

Taking the seven prisoners to a nearby grove of trees, the posse managed to get confessions out of a handful of them before they hanged the whole group. The *Weekly State Gazette* identified the seven as horse thieves named "J.T. Sherrill, N.C. Vivion, Wm. Hester, Dr. Jno. W. Walker and his three sons, Francis, Thos. and Jacob Walker." The bodies were left lying on the ground or hanging from the trees before finally being buried by a white couple and various enslaved people sent by other locals who did not care to bury the men themselves. At least four of the seven were buried in a common grave underneath the hanging tree, with no marker.[165]

## Belton Jail Murders, 1874

A decade later, the citizens of Belton enacted their own extrajudicial justice on prisoners in their town. The Belton Jail was only a year old in 1874 and was already quite full. On May 25, the prisoners included eight alleged horse thieves and a man who was accused of murdering his wife with an axe.

When the sheriff left town for a bit, local vigilantes decided to get take matters into their own hands. A mob formed. Just how many individuals made up that mob is unknown, but estimates range from three to five hundred.

"Once news spread throughout the state, it can be assumed that people wanted to enforce justice," executive director of the Bell County Museum, Coleman Hampton, told KXXV 25. "The mob broke in and according to the two prisoners who were not harmed, the prisoners were questioned and then shot and killed by the mob."[166]

The murdered men included William Henry Grumbles, John Alexander, Loyd Coleman, J.S. McDonald, Marion McDonald and William S. Smith. Only the last names of three of the victims are known: Bicknel, Cowen and Crow. The mob dragged the bodies just outside of the jail and left them there.

On May 26, 1874, the Belton court budgeted $70.55 for the cost of burial for the nine prisoners "recently killed in the county jail," with an additional $15.00 for "superintending" the burial. While a mass grave was planned for the men, one version of the story says a judge allowed the extra effort of single graves, although it's not clear which sort of burial the men ended

The imposing building that housed the Bell County Jail in Belton is still standing. Built in 1873, only one year later, a vigilante mob overran the jail and murdered nine prisoners. *Author's collection.*

up receiving. In September 1874, the court also "allowed $6 for painting the names of the nine murdered prisoners on their headboards."[167] Those headboards are no longer there, but a headstone believed to be located near the grave is engraved "Belton Jail Prisoners" followed by their death dates and all nine of their last names.

## THE HASSELL MURDERS, 1926

Most times it is not murderers who end up in a mass grave, but their victims. One notorious killer left multiple mass graves in his wake, including one of nine people in Texas, before he was finally apprehended.

Death seemed to follow George Hassell everywhere he went. Around 1917, his common-law wife and her three adopted children died in his home in Whittier, California. Then, in 1924, having moved to Oklahoma, George was working in a field with his brother Thomas when the latter suffered a terrible accident, kicked to death by a mule.

Perhaps united by their grief at this unexpected and violent loss, George and his brother's widow, Susan Hassell, married and moved with eight of her nine children to Farwell, Texas. But, seemingly, George's bad luck continued, and in 1926, he admitted to a neighbor that his wife had left him for another man and taken the kids.

In fact, George Hassell, who would soon be known as the "Texas wholesale murderer," had killed them all.[168] Within weeks of the Farwell slaughter, the law was closing in, and Hassell attempted suicide by stabbing himself in the chest as the sheriff's men were digging up his nine family members, whom he had dumped in a hole in the backyard of their home.[169] Later, the bodies of his four California victims were also discovered in a single grave under the house George lived at in that state while going by the alias "George Baker."

According to reports, George Hassell gave a lengthy confession from his hospital bed and/or his jail cell. This was read out at his trial. He claimed his mother had murdered his stepfather with poison when he was a teenager. He decided to kill her in turn but got too drunk to shoot her. He joined the army during World War I, which might have been the most legally acceptable outlet for his murderous urges, but he deserted.

George claimed he hadn't meant to kill Susan but that after an argument over his raping and impregnating his thirteen-year-old adopted daughter/niece, he got drunk and then murdered Susan with a hammer. He then proceeded to go room to room, killing the children, using multiple weapons, including a straight razor, stockings, a gun and an axe. One of their eight children—Alton, the oldest at twenty-one—was away, and George waited three days for him to return home and then murdered him as well.

George Hassell was found guilty of the murder of Alton and was sentenced to die in the electric chair. His sentence was carried out on February 10, 1928, in Huntsville. It took eight minutes and three shocks of electricity

This notorious image of family annihilator George Hassell came about while he was waiting to be sentenced. Hassell originally posed for the photographer with a serious face, and a reporter for the *Amarillo News-Globe* said to him, "George, you say you aren't worried about what is going to happen to you. Let's see you laugh." The murderer was more than happy to do so. *Amarillo Public Library Photoarchive Collection.*

for George to die. He was thirty-nine. His gravestone notes he was the thirty-seventh convict executed in the state of Texas.

As for the Farwell victims, they were removed from their makeshift mass grave on their farm and buried together in Olivet Cemetery. While technically buried next to each other in a single plot, they share a common gravestone. The *Winslow Daily Mail* reported that the entire community turned out to mourn the family and that every able-bodied man present helped dig the graves.

Texas Historical Commission Marker Number 14559 notes the presence of the mass burial, saying the family was murdered in a "local tragedy."[170]

## THE SLOCUM MASSACRE, 1910

No one knows what set off the Slocum Massacre, a frenzied and indiscriminate killing spree of Black residents of Slocum and the surrounding area on July 29 and 30, 1910. But then, there didn't need to be a reason. Black people living in white spaces was enough, with rumors and fearmongering to help the violence along.

The story of the massacre made news across the country. A *New York Times* story on August 1 quoted an eyewitness who painted a haunting picture of the savagery: "Men were going about killing negroes as fast as they could find them, and so far as I was able to ascertain, without any real cause. These negroes have done no wrong that I could discover. There was just a hotheaded gang hunting them down and killing them. I don't know how many were in the mob, but I think there must have been 200 or 300. Some of them cut telephone wires. They hunted the negroes down like sheep."[171]

It is worth noting that even if someone of any race *has* "done wrong," it is still illegal for vigilante mobs to extrajudicially murder them.

Reporting at the time placed the number of victims at anywhere between eighteen and forty, but the true scope of the carnage would only become clear over time. While exact numbers will never be known, research has revealed that an estimate of two hundred victims of the mob is probably a conservative one.

An August 1, 1910 article in the *Houston Post* explained how the many, many dead were disposed of by a Black population still in fear for their lives: "Many of the bodies were in a state of decomposition, and the action was taken as a measure to ensure public health. A trench twelve feet in depth had been dug during the early hours of the day and in this ditch, the bodies were placed and

The hard-won marker recognizing the Slocum Massacre downplays the horror of the events, naming the eight confirmed victims but failing to mention the estimated two-hundred-plus other murders. *Renelibrary/ Wikimedia Commons (Creative Commons Attribution-Share Alike 4.0 International license).*

covered. In many cases, relatives of the Negroes discovered the whereabouts of a body and dragged it to a secluded spot during the hours of the night."[172]

The stories of these mass burials were passed down to the next generations. In 2016, Michael Vickery told the *Washington Post* that when he was a child his grandfather pointed to a spot under an oak tree still scarred with buckshot and told him that there were eight Black people "buried in one hole right here."[173]

The Slocum Massacre, or Slocum Race Riot, may be the most repulsive hate crime ever to happen on Texas soil. This reality has made it hard for descendants of those who were targeted to convince some modern Texans that the event and their ancestors deserve to be remembered and memorialized, no matter how painful it is to reflect on the evil that took place.

Constance Hollie-Jawaid's great-great-grandfather Jack Holley was a survivor of the Slocum Massacre. She has been one of the leading voices fighting for acknowledgment of the atrocity, which the Texas legislature finally undertook in 2011. And she is very clear about the obvious double standard applied to the victims of this crime. "There are people out there, not just my relatives, but people who descend from these victims and their bodies are still buried," she told the *Palestine Herald-Press* in 2021. "I feel like if I call the Governor of Texas right now and said, 'sir, we have found a mass grave of Confederate soldiers...,' they would be exhumed by noon. But because they are Black it doesn't matter."[174]

After a long, hard and controversial campaign, a historical marker about the massacre was finally erected in Slocum in 2016. However, as there is limited information on where the mass graves are located, the site is not connected to the memories of the victims as much as one might hope.

In 2016, Hollie-Jawaid explained to the *Tyler Morning Herald*: "We want access to these locations to discover [the] mass graves so their souls can be reunited with family and for them to have a proper burial,"[175] and not remain forever, as she put it in a 2019 interview with the *Texas Observer*, "piled upon one another in a mass grave, like dogs."[176]

## The Porvenir Massacre, 1918

The February 8, 1918 edition of the *El Paso Morning Times* ran a front-page story on a vicious, premeditated crime perpetrated by a posse of Texas lawmen on Mexican immigrants in the small border town of Porvenir on January 28. The details were enough to strike fear into anyone: "Men were dragged from their beds, and, without having been given time to dress, were led away in their nightclothes to the edge of the settlement, where they were shot to death by the posse. The bodies of the men were found the next day where they had fallen, riddled with bullets."[177]

The reason for these murders was the men's alleged involvement in a raid on the nearby Brite Ranch the previous December, where bandits stole thousands of dollars and killed three people. But there was absolutely no reason for the posse that murdered the men of Porvenir to think they had anything to do with it—other than racist assumptions about them because of their ethnicity. These were innocent men, victims of cold-blooded murder.

The posse left the bodies of the fifteen men they killed lying in the desert. It was later revealed by a witness that once the bodies were discovered, Colonel George Langhorne was ordered to "send soldiers to bury the dead Mexicans, which he did not do." Instead, it was left to the families of the dead men to dispose of their remains; "the Mexicans carried them across the river and buried them in Mexico."[178]

**BAND OF 15 MEXICANS KILLED BY RANGERS**

**Bodies Were Then Taken Across the Border for Burial.**

**U. S. Soldiers Had Nothing to Do With Affair at Porvenir—Protest Has Been Made to Washington.**

(*Associated Press Report.*)

MARFA, Texas, Feb. 7.—Texas Rangers reported on January 31 that they had had trouble with a band of Mexicans at Porvenir, who were supposed to have been implicated in the Brite ranch raid. They admitted having killed 15 of the number. The bodies were taken across the Rio Grande to El Comidor and buried by their families and friends.

The United States Army had nothing to do with the affair and no soldiers were near that place the night of the killings. Instead, a number of Mexicans sought and received protection from the military at Everett's ranch, the military authorities here said.

Press reports at the time illustrate how the massacre was seen for the crime it was. This Associated Press article does not take the Texas Rangers' rationale for the murders at face value and makes clear the U.S. Army was anxious to distance itself from the deadly event. *Renelibrary/Wikimedia Commons (Creative Commons Attribution-Share Alike 4.0 International license).*

In January 1919, in response to the Porvenir Massacre and thousands of other murders believed to be the work of the Texas Rangers, Texas state representative José T. Canales of Brownsville filed nineteen charges against the organization. As part of the investigations and inquiries that followed, the wives of the murdered men were interviewed about that night. Their experiences were alarmingly similar. There was no warning, no explanation and no way to refuse. White men simply broke into their homes in the dead of night and took their husbands away—husbands who never came home.

One woman, through a translator, told her story:

> *My husband and I with our family of four children have lived in Porvenir for one year and four months; That my husband was an American citizen; That about January 19, 1918, near midnight, three men came in my house, told my husband to get up and go with them; that they did not offer him violence in the house, and I did not know why they were taking him out; That about thirty minutes after they left my house I heard many guns being discharged; That the next morning I learned that my husband had been killed by being shot at a point very near my house. Other men of Porvenir were killed at the same time and place as my husband, which was around a little hill and about three minutes walk from my house.*[179]

Despite the official inquiries and minor career repercussions for some of those involved in the Porvenir Massacre, the event was almost completely forgotten, except by those who lived there at the time. Many relatives of the survivors say they never spoke about it, or if they did, they were not believed, because the crime was so heinous it didn't seem like it could be true. It didn't help that records of the murders were few and far between.

"Nobody went to the courthouse in Marfa to file a death certificate," Jerry Patterson, a former land commissioner and state senator, told the *Big Bend Sentinel* in 2021. "There wasn't anybody left around to do it."[180]

The mass grave of the victims of the Porvenir Massacre is an outlier here, in that it lies just on the other side of the Mexican border, and therefore does not fit this book's self-imposed requirements of a Texas mass grave. But the crime that resulted in the mass burial took place on Texas soil, was committed by Texans and, unfortunately, has seen an attempted cover-up by modern Texans who do not want their families or their local area tied to such a vicious crime. It is therefore important for Texans to remember the reason for the mass grave that is barely a mile away from their home.

# V

# THE UNKNOWN DEAD

For some, a mass grave is not the final indignity. For some, they not only go to their grave in the company of others but also without any record of who they were. Nameless, their existence is lost to history.

## 12

# THE TRULY UNKNOWN

While the names of those who end their days in a mass grave are frequently absent, oftentimes, at least some information can be gleaned about them. They were a soldier fighting for the Union in the Civil War or a member of the Webster Wagon Train, for example. But then there are the mass graves that reveal almost nothing about those who ended up there.

## Rockport

In 1980, construction workers were surprised to uncover a mass grave of a dozen skeletons in Rockport, Texas. The owner of the land, Stephen Stanick, was flummoxed. "I don't have the slightest idea what it is," he told UPI. "There were no artifacts. Nothing in there to tell you who the people were."[181] This did not keep him from guessing they might have been victims of pirates.

## Concordia Cemetery, El Paso

The Chinese community in El Paso in the late 1800s flourished, even as the United States closed its borders to individuals from China. Living and dying in their new home, a section of El Paso's Concordia Cemetery was dedicated to Chinese burials. But their ethnicity is the only thing known about those interred in a common grave there. On top of a low, wide, gray rock tomb is a small marker reading, in Chinese characters, "Grave of deceased friends, renovated in Joong Choon [the second lunar month] of the year Yuet Gee [1965], repainted in 1993."[182] The names, ages, genders and even the number of people laid to rest there are unknown.

## EMIGRANT CROSSING

To the east of El Paso, immigrants and emigrants of any nationality had to ford the treacherous Pecos River. There were only a few spots where it was safe to do so. One, in Pecos, Texas, known as Emigrant Crossing, was popular in 1849 for prospectors heading west, hoping to make their fortune in the California Gold Rush.[183]

In 1924, a man walked into the sheriff's department with a skull he'd found less than a mile downstream of the ford. A group went to investigate the location, including Barney Hubbs, who told his version of the story in 1992.

Hubbs said the men "dug up 18 skeletons, just a mass burial there....They had been just stuffed in there, you know, no protection on the bodies....The coyotes had dug up their skeletons."

They found evidence the group was part of a wagon train and concluded the group was killed in a clash with Native Americans, but there is no evidence of this. Hobbs explained, "The supposition is—and most of it is supposition—that...they were emigrants, and they were crossing the river at Emigrant Crossing, and the Indians attacked them and killed [them] all."[184]

It is possible the remains belonged to a party of surveyors who were also said to have been killed fighting Native Americans in the area in the 1870s. It should be noted, however, that if it was a clash with a local tribe, it would have been one of the largest massacres of white people involving Native Americans in the history of Texas—and was somehow completely overlooked or forgotten.

## GONZALES

Gonzales was no stranger to the idea of mass burials, as the historical marker erected in the town's cemetery in 1966 attests: "By tradition, remains of early settlers buried at first in cemetery square, inner town of Gonzales, rest here in a common grave."[185]

As noted in the introduction, local folklore is not always correct when it comes to remembering who is buried where, and like Matagorda, Gonzales may not have the grave it thinks it does in that location. However, perhaps the settlers, if they are there, should consider themselves lucky they have not been found, considering what happened when the town discovered a different mass grave in 1905.

Workers preparing to lay a foundation for a warehouse discovered a long trench full of human bones. The *Gonzales Inquirer* described the scene: "Protruding from either side of the excavation could be seen pieces of ribs, skulls, thigh bones, etc....In one place were noticed two skulls lying close together, the remains extending in opposite directions, while above both were seen the remains of others."

Despite the paper estimating the grave once held the bodies of up to nineteen people, those two skulls were the only ones found. Of those, only one was fully intact, but rather than give it a proper burial, the newspaper had less reverent plans, letting readers know the skull "is now on exhibition in the office, where it has been viewed by a number of people. The skull is rather small, with retreating forehead, and is of unusual thickness. The teeth are in a fair state of preservation."[186]

Writer Murray Montgomery researched this mysterious mass grave extensively but has been thwarted in his attempts to discover anything about the remains found there.[187] The residents of Gonzales in 1905 were apparently uninterested in the discovery of one-and-a-half dozen bodies, and no further excavation was done. Even the anonymous skull in the newspaper office vanished. Whoever was buried in that mass grave, their names and the events that led to them ending up there have been lost to history.

# TURKEY CREEK

The same fate befell the nineteen bodies discovered in one grave on Turkey Creek, about three miles from Christine, Texas. In a 1927 article, the *Frontier Times* reported that farmer W.G. Wiley was digging a hole for a water tank when he uncovered the mass grave. "After discovery of the first skeleton, further investigation was made, and eighteen additional skeletons were found lying in a tunnel grave about three feet deep, and with the exception of two of the bodies which were piled cross-wise, as if they had been hurriedly thrown into the grave, all were placed in regular order, and were with the head to the east."

It appeared the bodies had been burned, but it was still possible to estimate that the grave held the remains of at least eighteen adults and one infant. Once again, witnesses concluded that they must have been white settlers killed in a clash with Native Americans, which is, of course, just one of many possibilities.

The people of Christine were more intrigued by their mass grave discovery than were those of Gonzales, and men, women and children turned out to continue digging and look for more clues. However, as the *Frontier Times* poignantly notes, "Nothing has been discovered, however, which might reveal the identity of the ill-fated settlers and it is believed that they will be nameless forevermore."[188]

## San Jose Cemetery I and II, Austin

An "orphaned" cemetery is one where no official body takes responsibility for it any longer. In the Montopolis neighborhood of Austin, two orphaned cemeteries, San Jose I and II, have drawn the interest of local residents, local historians and researchers from the University of Texas at Austin. As well as contributing to the upkeep of the burial grounds, these groups have started investigating who is buried in the many unmarked graves.

In 2021, Diana Hernandez, lead researcher and founder of (Re)Claiming Memories, told FOX 7, "We found some aerial footage historic aerial footage [*sic*] from the '50s where you could see what looks to be like trenches and we really believe that the trenches were used for a pandemic burials [*sic*]."[189] Hernandez believes these burials coincide with epidemics that occurred in the 1930s and '40s.

But while there have been many breakthroughs on individual burials, the identities of those in these mass graves are lost forever. That same year, in an interview with NPR station KUT 90.5, Hernandez said that during epidemics, "They were getting so many bodies that they were burying people in layers on top of each other, and they stopped documenting who all was getting buried. Because there's no documentation for the number of layers for the people that were being buried in these mass graves, we're just never going to know. There's going to be layers of people that we're never going to be able to identify."[190]

The entrance to San Jose Cemetery I in Austin. *Scott218/Wikimedia Commons (Creative Commons Attribution-Share Alike 4.0 International license).*

Most, if not all, of the individuals buried in these cemeteries were people of color, specifically those of Mexican descent. Racist feelings meant that even in death, white people did not want to share the same space with people of color and forced them to build their own separate cemeteries.

# 13

# THE DISINTERRED OR DISREGARDED

**N**ot all of the anonymous dead buried in mass graves started out that way. In some cases, bodies were buried in single graves with reverence and honor and then, by action or accident, their remains were disinterred and became part of a group burial, at which point their identifying information was lost.

## CEDAR GROVE CEMETERY, SANDERSON

On June 11, 1965, a colossal flood brought on by eleven inches of rain washed half of Sanderson, Texas, away. All told, twenty-six people died and millions of dollars in damage occurred. The rush of water means some people were searching for loved ones for days and bodies were found up to five miles away.

Yet it managed, somehow, to get worse. Two of the town's cemeteries were so badly flooded that bodies buried long before were unearthed and deposited around town. Curator of the Terrell County Memorial Museum, Bill Smith, told NewsWest9 in 2015, "So we were faced with not only looking for flood victims, but they also would come across cadavers from the cemetery."[191]

The combination of water and bodies was a public health emergency, and something had to be done about it. On June 14, 1965, the *El Paso Herald-Post* reported that just one day after the flood, "bodies washed out of the Sanderson Cemetery were mass-buried in a bulldozed pit to eliminate additional health hazards."[192]

Exactly ten years to the day after the flood, Terrell County residents erected a large stone monument over the mass grave in Sanderson's Cedar Grove Cemetery. It reads, "A common grave of those disinterred by floodwaters of June 11, 1965."[193]

## San Antonio National Cemetery

One of the risks of being a soldier is that you may die far from home. While the U.S. military makes it a rule to bring every fallen soldier home, this was much more difficult in the period before refrigeration or widespread embalming. This meant the only way to safely "store" remains until they could be moved to an appropriate resting place was to bury them near where they fell.

When the San Antonio National Cemetery was created in 1867, members of the military buried in the city and at other, more far-flung rural locations,

The gravestone for the unknown soldiers in San Antonio National Cemetery. When thirty-five of those buried in the mass grave were identified, a plaque was added to the base of the memorial in 1992 listing their names, dates and ranks. *Author's collection*.

were relocated there. However, information about the deceased was often lost by that point. Over three hundred unknown soldiers lie in a common grave in the cemetery's Section H, with a large gravestone commemorating them nearby.[194]

Some names of those buried there are known, even if they cannot be directly connected to a specific set of remains. Private William H. Barnes was born into enslavement before fighting for the Union in the Civil War. He was the first Black U.S. soldier awarded the Medal of Honor.[195] After his death from tuberculosis in 1866, he was buried in Indianola. By the time his and other bodies were moved to San Antonio a couple of years later, his grave marker was gone, meaning he could not be positively identified and is buried with the unknowns.[196]

## POOR FARMS

Modern Texans would probably be surprised to know that mass burials still occur with regularity, right in their towns and counties. This is shocking, since the stories of mass graves feel like they are rooted firmly in the past, during the time of the frontier and wars that took place domestically.

But as Timothy W. Wolfe and Clifton D. Bryant, writing in 2003, explain in the *Handbook of Death & Dying*, in American society "we do tolerate mass burial for the indigent, as in the case of Potter's Field."[197] One only has to look at how local governments treat the homeless or other poor folks in need to know that, for some, they become unworthy of the basic respect all humans are owed. In life, this might mean designing benches so they cannot lie down or making camping illegal. In death, it means the poor or unhoused often go to their graves with many others who cannot afford a private burial or whose bodies are never claimed by loved ones.

Poor farms, places for those in dire circumstances to go in order to survive, if barely, may not exist anymore, but they left behind reminders in their cemeteries. But it seems that the poor can inconvenience the living even when they are dead.

In 1885, Johnson County purchased land southwest of Cleburne and established the County Farm, a home for the elderly, paupers and the "feeble-minded."[198] Those who lived there had no other options—they were desperate. In exchange for a roof over their heads and three square meals, they agreed to work the farm and gave up control of "their personal lives and basic rights as a citizen, including their right to vote."[199]

Records from 1903 show the county contracted a local undertaker to bury anyone who died at the farm for a flat fee of $7.50, including a "grade 0" coffin. There were no headstones, just wood stakes marking each grave.

The County Farm closed down in 1944, and the land was sold. In 1963, plans for a dam that would flood the area necessitated the disinterment of seventy-two burials from the farm cemetery. They were reinterred in a common grave in Rose Hill Cemetery with no marker.

The Travis County Poor Farm was established around 1883 and shuttered fifty years later. In the 1930s, the land, now Tarrytown, was sold to a developer. The remains of an estimated one hundred to two hundred residents of the farm were moved to the Travis International Cemetery. There they were forgotten about. In July 1967, the *Austin American-Statesman* called out the lack of respect for those buried there under the headline "a disgrace…," calling the cemetery "prestigious in name only" and looking "more like a goat pasture than a final resting place."[200] This shamed the county commissioner into cleaning it up.

Harris County opened its second poor farm in 1894, and it was in use until 1922. When the seventy-five residents living there were moved to an "old folks' home," the remains of those in the poor farm cemetery were also moved to the new location, where they were "dumped in a common grave."[201] Why did the graves need to be disturbed? Because the land was— you guessed it—sold to developers.

Bexar County was ahead of the game when it came to digging up poor people to make a buck. In 1909, the county judge tried to sell the land that housed the county's poor farm and pauper cemetery, but the offers weren't as much as anticipated. Four years later, the judge believed that by "doing away with the unsightly burying ground," the land "should bring a good sum." The county contracted with an undertaker to remove the remains and bury the unknown dead in a common grave at the new poor farm, assuring the readers of the *San Antonio Light* that they would dig "suitable shafts."[202]

## Phillips Memorial Cemetery, Texas City

The burial grounds of people of color, particularly Blacks, both before and after the Civil War, are some of the most endangered in Texas. The reasons for this could fill their own book, but in more recent years, the problem is the disregard for these cemeteries when they are rediscovered.

An 1860 painting of the funeral for an enslaved person on the Louisiana plantation of former governor of Mississippi Tilghman Tucker gives a sense of what large, emotional events they could be for those held in bondage. Many of these burial grounds have been lost or destroyed. *Historic New Orleans Collection/Bridgeman Images.*

The Phillips Memorial Cemetery in Texas City was founded by formerly enslaved people in the 1870s. But by the 1920s, the city had decided that the cemetery was inconveniently located for its development plans.

A colorful and informative marker erected in the cemetery by the 1867 Settlement Historic District and Texas City explains: "In 1927, the state of Texas rerouted Highway 6 to the cemetery's side of the GH&H tracks. The new highway went through the oldest section of the cemetery, and tragically the bodies were taken from their caskets and placed in a common grave behind the latest gravesites."[203]

While as many as five bodies may have been reinterred in a mass grave, a highway expansion in 1991 discovered that, in fact, the disregard for the dead was far worse than that: most of the bodies near the road's proposed path were not relocated at all. Construction crews were shocked when their equipment uncovered "funerary hardware and human remains."[204]

## Holy Cross Cemetery, San Antonio

Amos Jackson was a Buffalo Soldier and after the Civil War was one of the first formerly enslaved individuals to purchase his own land in the San Antonio area. Eventually, the interrelated Jackson, Winters and Anthony families purchased adjoining farms. On a shared piece of land they started a family cemetery. When Amos Jackson died, he was buried there under a large monument.

By 1986, however, that land was owned by a development company, and the cemetery was now inconvenient. So without contacting any of the relatives of those buried there, the company disinterred the remains and moved them to Holy Cross Cemetery. They were buried in a common grave under a single stone on which only six names were recorded. The marker notes there are also sixty-six unknowns in the grave. The Jackson family cemetery had at least one hundred burials in it, and it is not known what happened to the other bodies.

Landscape architect and historian Everett Fly, a former member of San Antonio's Historic and Design Review Commission, made plain the shameful truth to KSAT News in 2017: "They weren't moved really to protect them. It was just to get them out of the way."[205]

"The descendants seemed upset that the landowners moved [remains from] the cemetery without their consent," Brother Ed Loch, archivist for the Catholic Archdiocese of San Antonio, told the *San Antonio Express-News* in 2018. "My hunch is that the owners wanted to get rid of the cemetery quickly and without much fanfare."[206]

A representative for the then-owner of the former cemetery, Fasken Oil and Ranch Ltd., claimed the company was told by Holy Cross staff that the bodies had not been interred in a mass grave but in twenty graves with "no more than four buried together in a single grave. Where there were reported to be kin, the parties were buried together. When a headstone was present, it was relocated and buried with the body of the deceased."[207]

As Fly wryly pointed out, "When you start stacking, to me that's a mass grave."[208]

# 14

# INDUSTRIAL ACCIDENTS
# AND THE TOLL OF NEGLECT

## Penwell, 1881

Only a few feet away from a railroad track near Penwell, Ector County, is one of the most perplexing mass graves in Texas. At the end of an unpaved road, just to the side of the tracks on land still owned by the railroad, is a long pile of white stones marked with a cross. The cross reads, "five chinamen died while building railroad…common grave."[209] The grave site itself is neat and well cared for; considering the remote location, it is notable that the Texas & Pacific Railway Company has maintained the site for well over a century.

Mel Brown, author of *Chinese Heart of Texas: The San Antonio Community (1875–1975)*, has done extensive research on this grave. It is believed the men died in a dynamite explosion and were buried head to toe in the grave, hence the unusual length of the stone pile atop it.

Nothing else is known about this common grave or the men laid to rest there, but there are likely other mass graves of Chinese men who came to Texas to work on the railroads in the 1800s. Brown mentions epidemics that killed many of the immigrants and that railroad company policy at the time was to bury victims together at the side of the tracks, as in Penwell. However, any other mass graves of those from this marginalized population have since been lost.

## Emporia, 1906

The late Bob Bowman, former president of the East Texas Historical Association, covered the mystery of the Emporia sawmill disaster in his syndicated newspaper column. Emporia, now part of Diboll in Angelina County, was settled in 1892. Within three years it was a center for the lumber business, with two sawmills—the Emporia Sawmill and the Southern Pine Lumber Company—and a railroad line for shipping their products throughout the state.

The town's population boomed to 300 residents, with 125 of them employed either at one of the mills or on logging crews to supply the mills with raw material. But while the owners of the mills were rich, important men, the employees' living and working conditions seem to have been an afterthought.

Early on, there were signs the old Emporia mill was headed for disaster. A fire in 1897 burned it to the ground, seemingly (and miraculously) with no casualties. It was rebuilt three years later, but the owners were unconcerned

A sawmill in Wells, Texas, about twenty-five miles from where the Emporia Sawmill was located, pictured in 1939. Clearly, these types of buildings were little more than organized piles of tinder once a fire started. *New York Public Library.*

about the very real possibility the same thing could happen again—with deadly consequences. In a time long before the Occupational Safety and Health Administration (OSHA), this was almost homicidal negligence, since a newspaper report in 1904 noted water was scarce in the area, and to run the mill, water had to be hauled from a mile away. If another fire broke out, there would be no means to extinguish it.

In March 1906, the inevitable happened. A second fire engulfed the mill, killing over thirty employees. While there is not a lot of documentation about the disaster, it's believed most of the dead were African Americans. Unable to be identified because of their burns, the victims are said to have been buried in a mass grave. It was left unmarked.

The location of the grave has long been lost to history. (Indeed, it's not even clear where the old Emporia Sawmill was located.) Bowman writes that it is "rumored to lie somewhere east of U.S. 59 in Diboll's South Meadow area."[210]

There is always hope that, if this tragedy did indeed happen, the mass grave of the disregarded Black workers will be found, even accidentally.

## The Texas City Disaster, 1947

When a fire broke out onboard a ship in the Texas City port on April 16, 1947, no one thought much of it. The industrial city was used to fires on ships. Some people even wandered down to the docks to enjoy the excitement.

Then, the 2,300 tons of ammonium nitrate the ship was carrying ignited. The resulting explosion instantly killed an estimated 581 people, leveled one thousand buildings and was loud enough to terrify people more than ten miles away.

But the disaster was far from over. The fire spread, and fifteen hours after the first blast, another ship exploded, causing even more damage. It would be weeks before all the fires that began that day were finally extinguished.

Identifying the bodies of the hundreds of people who died was a monumental task. J.H. Arnette, the chief chemist for the Texas Department of Public Safety, explained the process to—of all things—a Rotary Club luncheon in September of that year. He called it "like working on a jig-saw puzzle." Every possible technique was used to glean to whom each set of remains belonged. "We learned how to treat the flesh of persons who had been burned so that fingerprints could be brought out," he said.[211]

The Texas City explosion and fires left buildings nothing but charred, twisted frames. An inscription on the back of this photo identifies the location as "Old Sugar Mill now Rubber Plant by Slip #1." Before the explosion, boxcars waited on the train tracks in front of the building. They were completely obliterated. *University of Houston Libraries Special Collections*.

The attempts were remarkably successful considering the difficulties involved. In the end, sixty-two unidentified bodies were buried in a mass grave in what is now the Texas City Memorial Park.

## THE GULF HOTEL FIRE, HOUSTON, 1943

During World War II, if you got off the bus in Houston with little money in your pocket and nowhere to stay (and you were a man), there was a good chance you'd end up down the street at the Gulf Hotel. It was a cheap place to lay your head down, it was nearby and it was seemingly never fully booked. That might be because the proprietors found ways to squeeze more and more men into the limited rooms. A cot for the night cost just twenty cents.

Just after midnight on September 7, 1943, an errant cigarette set a mattress on fire. As the flames raced through the building, men panicked and tried to escape, but the emergency exit lights were not working. Many jumped to their deaths from the upper floors. One man was hit by a falling window.

When the flames were extinguished, fifty-five men were dead. It is still the deadliest fire in Houston's history. Almost two dozen of those men were never identified or claimed by family members. Besides the issues of identification caused by the fire itself, the anonymous nature of the hotel also contributed to the difficulty in determining the victims' identities.

"Nobody in their family necessarily knows they're even staying in that hotel, or may not know they're in Houston," Brady Hutchison, a history instructor at Wharton County Junior College, told KPRC 2 Houston in 2018. "All their families knew was, 'my son, or my uncle, they left to go to Houston to look for work and we just never heard from them again.'"[212]

Almost three hundred mourners turned out to witness the funeral of thirty-six of the victims. Only fifteen of those had been identified. All were buried in one long trench in South Park Cemetery.

"They buried 21 unidentified people here," Hutchison reflected.[213]

A report in the September 8, 1943 edition of the *Houston Chronicle* took a more poignant tone than one might expect from a newspaper:

> *Who were these men? What strange, pathetic, colorful or drab histories led to a fate that sent them unrecognized to this tragic grave? Histories that shall be forever unwritten, untold.*
>
> *Some of them had good jobs, as shipyard workers, defense plant workers. Some, perhaps, were newspaper vendors, peddlers or clerks in hide away stores. Or were they beggars and crippled derelicts wandering in city streets with nothing to do, no place to go but their cots in the crowded hotel? What kind of homes did they come from? Where?*
>
> *No one will ever know.*[214]

# SUGAR LAND

Everyone knows that Abraham Lincoln freed enslaved Blacks with the Emancipation Proclamation. And Juneteeth celebrates the last people held in bondage in the United States, on Galveston, learning they were free. Then it was all made official with the Fourteenth and Fifteenth Amendments to the Constitution.

It's a nice story, and a simple one, which is, of course, why it's all wrong. For all intents and purposes, the enslaving of Black people in the South did not end until well into the twentieth century. As the iconic Black historian W.E.B. Du Bois lyrically put it, "The slave went free; stood a brief moment in the sun; then moved back again toward slavery."[215]

There were a variety of ways the post-Reconstruction South managed to get away with this, but one significant one was the use of prison labor. Society accepts, in general, that prisoners have very few rights. By arresting Black men on the slightest of charges, or for no reason at all, a steady supply of free labor was available through the prison system for those unethical enough to take advantage of it.

"It resembled slavery in every regard. It used the same commercial systems of slavery. It used all the same tactics of torture and compulsion and coercion, the same sexual exploitation of women," said Douglas Blackmon, author of the Pulitzer Prize–winning book *Slavery by Another Name: The Re-Enslavement of Black Americans from the Civil War to World War Two*. "It was explicitly established to recreate something as close to slavery as possible but using the criminal justice system."[216] In his book, he quotes Black prisoners' thoughts and feelings about their conditions. It was clear their lives were hellish. They were fed "food buzzards would not eat," knew they would spend "the prime of [their] life…as a slave" and were effectively "buried alive….Dead to the world."[217]

Black prisoners are pictured picking potatoes about 1909 while white men on horseback stand guard. It is a visual that is indistinguishable from half a century earlier. The Library of Congress records that these men may have been incarcerated at the Imperial State Prison Farm, the same facility where the Sugar Land mass grave victims were held. *Library of Congress.*

Folksinger James "Iron Head" Baker is pictured in 1934 when he was about sixty-four years old. A nonviolent criminal, he'd been in and out of the Imperial State Prison Farm for decades and would have been there when many of those in the Sugar Land mass grave were buried. *Library of Congress.*

In many cases, prisoners found themselves literally dead as well. The horrible conditions and disregard for any humanity of the men meant deaths were common.

"When the state leased convicts out to private contractors, they had no financial interest in the health or welfare of the people working for them," W. Caleb McDaniel, a history professor at Rice University in Houston, explained to the *Washington Post* in 2016. "And so the convict-leasing system saw extremely high levels of mortality and sickness under convict lessees. If the prisoner died, they would simply go back to the state and say, 'You owe us another prisoner.'"[218]

Texas was home to many prisons that were part of this system. However, no one expected a mass burial site of convicts incarcerated at the Imperial State Prison Farm to reemerge during the construction of a new building at a school in Sugar Land. The remains of ninety-five men were recovered, many of whom showed signs of debilitating injuries from their forced labor. The graves also produced chains. However, there were no markers or other indications of who these men were, besides being prisoners who were likely worked to death.

"No other burial ground like this has been found," McDaniel told *USA Today* in 2018. "The history of convict leasing is really important for

Americans today to understand. It reminds us of how resilient racism was after the Civil War and the end of slavery, and it's a reminder we still need in the present."[219]

# Migrants, 2014

"Nobody cares about dead immigrants," Dr. Lori Baker, a forensic anthropologist at Baylor University, said. "They're invisible when they're alive, and they're even more invisible when they're dead."[220]

But Baker made it her mission to give names back to migrants who died while trying to make it to safety in Texas. In 2013, she and her students were working at Sacred Heart Cemetery in Brooks County, exhuming bodies under markers that read only "Unknown" or "Skeletal Remains" in order to collect DNA samples to use in identification.

Instead of the ten or so bodies Baker expected in the graves, she discovered more than fifty shoved into the same amount of space. Some were still in body bags. Returning the next summer, she and her students found seventy more bodies buried in mass graves. The remains were in plastic kitchen bags, burlap sacks and even a milk crate. Bodies were piled up to five deep in a single grave.

The discovery made national news, and State Senator Juan "Chuy" Hinojosa demanded an investigation into how the disrespectful mass burials happened. "This is too serious of a wrongdoing," he said. "I'm appalled at the number of bodies just left in body bags and, in many instances, more than one body in one bag."[221]

Dr. Baker told a meeting of county officials about what she and her students had discovered. "There were many more burials than there were grave markers. Many graves did not have markers, some graves had multiple markers but only one individual and many graves had one marker and multiple individuals in the grave."[222]

During a press conference on a visit to McAllen on June 23, 2014, Governor Rick Perry was asked about the discovery of the mass graves and if he thought the law needed to be changed to keep it from happening again. He said, "Certainly if there is evidence of criminal wrongdoing, it should be investigated and that would be left up to the appropriate law enforcement agency."[223] But when he was asked a virtually identical question at another Q&A on July 3, his answer had changed dramatically. Perry said, "These are not mass graves, but some gravesites with multiple remains in them that are being exhumed for identification."[224]

As sickening as the complete disregard for these migrants and their remains was, technically—if not morally—it appeared no law had been broken. Lieutenant Corey Lain, an investigator with the Texas Rangers, explained, "There are no statutes prohibiting more than one set of human remains to be buried with another at a government-owned cemetery" and "no Texas statutes that govern the burial proximity, or positioning limitations, in relation to other buried human remains." And since Texas law defined a casket simply as "a container used to hold the remains of a deceased person,"[225] disposing someone in a body bag or literally anything else was legal, no matter how insulting or disrespectful to their basic humanity.

At a 2015 meeting of Texas's Forensic Science Commission, State Representative Terry Canales took issue with Governor Perry's splitting hairs over terminology and what the discovery of the graves said about the people of Texas.

> *Last session we found that Brooks County was burying bodies in mass graves. There was a dispute whether you could consider it a mass grave by definition, but they were mass graves. Not only was that disturbing, but they also were unidentified. I thought about how people were sacrificing their lives to get here and would do anything to get here. We're that beautiful of a country, but we were still burying people in a mass grave. Mass graves is not us. It's not what Texans do or what Americans do.*[226]

"It's as if they never existed," Kate Spradley, a Texas State University biological anthropologist, told the *Houston Chronicle* in 2015. "Everyone has the right to be recognized as a person."[227]

# AUTHOR'S NOTE

I am not, as they say, from 'round here.

I identify as a Californian, albeit one by way of New Jersey, with a few years of "finding myself" in Europe in my mid-twenties thrown in for good measure.

So you can imagine my bewilderment when this slogan, on the billboard of a primary candidate who shall remain nameless, greeted me on a weekend getaway to Waco: "Send Californians back to California."

Regrettably, one comes to expect anti-immigrant sentiments from swathes of society, and it is certainly not limited to Texas. But the desire to send Americans back to where they came from—another part of America—was fresh enough to be shocking.

Yet, at the same time, it represents the same social conflicts that have defined the state from its beginning—and well before. Texans, or at least the people occupying the land that makes up the present-day state, have always defined themselves by the fact that other groups arrived here after they did, and those Johnny-come-latelies were the *real* unwelcome interlopers.

The Caddos did not want the Comanches here. None of the local Native American tribes wanted the Spanish or Mexicans here. Mexicans did not want Anglo settlers from the United States. The Confederates did not want the Union-supporting European immigrants. After the Civil War, free Blacks were unwelcome. And one needs only to watch certain news channels today to learn what Texans (allegedly) feel about the "invasion" on their southern border.

(Planet Earth is also not a huge fan of humanity as a whole, generally speaking, and as we have seenn, it has proven perfectly capable of being the reason for mass graves.)

With so many influxes of very different cultures fighting for their place, the history of Texas is exceptionally, perhaps even uniquely, messy. But for whatever reason, to truly be Texan, to express love and patriotism for one's state, means ignoring the darkest parts of history, or—even worse—warping them completely in an attempt to turn the bad things into good things.

In his book *Shadowed Ground: America's Landscapes of Violence and Tragedy*, Kenneth E. Foote writes:

> *By the time of the Centennial, Texas history had been smoothed and shaped effectively in all manner of literature and popular media. Historical scholarship, biography, textbooks, popular fiction, and movies all had the effect of accentuating the positive connotations of Texas history and muting the negative ones. The process involved simplifying the historical record to omit troublesome detail and shaping what remained into a wide range of myths and legends. By extending the peaks and bridging the troughs, Texas history became a curve arching ever upward towards progress, liberty, and freedom.*[228]

I began learning Texas history relatively late in life, having never been taught a single fact about the state in school, so I hope this allows me to see my beloved adopted home with clear eyes. What I did learn is that ignoring the horrors of the past simply leads to the same kind of suffering over and over and over again. Speaking about the Slocum Massacre, State Representative James White said, "Sometimes it may be extremely tough for local areas to deal with these issues, but the fact of the matter is we have a responsibility to history and to our legacy and making sure the story is told correctly and appropriately so it will be a lesson and also an inspiration for future generations of Texans."[229]

I hope this book lives up to that responsibility.

# NOTES

## *Introduction*

1. "Police to Search Texas Property for Possible Mass Grave," BBC News, June 8, 2011, www.bbc.com.
2. "Police Investigate Reports of Mass Grave with 'A Lot of Bodies' near Hardin, Texas," CBS News, June 8, 2011, www.cbsnews.com.
3. Manny Fernandez and Anahad O'Connor, "Mass Grave Report in Texas Proves False," *New York Times*, June 7, 2011.
4. The woman who called in the false tip would later be found guilty of making defamatory statements about the home's occupants and ordered to pay the couple $6.8 million. Carol Christian, "'Psychic' Who Reported Mass Grave North of Houston Must Pay $7 Million," *Houston Chronicle*, June 12, 2013.
5. Fernandez and O'Connor, "Mass Grave Report in Texas."
6. Clifton D. Bryant, ed., *Handbook of Death & Dying* (Thousand Oaks, CA: Sage Publications, 2003).

## *1. Yellow Fever*

7. Texas Department of State Health Service, "What You Need to Know About: Yellow Fever," https://www.dshs.state.tx.us.
8. "Yellow Fever" and "Yellow Fever News," *Austin American-Statesman*, October 25, 1873.
9. Mike Vance, "Texas Response to Yellow Fever in 19th Century Echoes Coronavirus Response Today," *Houston Chronicle*, May 1, 2020.

10. Historical Marker Database, "St. Peter Cemetery," https://www.hmdb.org.

11. Sherie Knape, "The 1867 Yellow Fever Epidemic," Fayette County TXGenWeb Project, web.archive.org/web/20200204072314/http://www.fayettecountyhistory.org/la_grange_yellow_fever.htm.

12. Ibid.

13. Historical Marker Database, "St. Peter Cemetery."

## 2. Cholera

14. An 1849 article describes the town of Roma on the Rio Grande as "totally deserted" and reported that in Brownsville, "not twenty persons were to be seen in a day's walk." *Corpus Christi Star*, "Cholera on the Rio Grande," March 31, 1849.

15. *Texian Advocate*, January 11, 1849.

16. Haggard, J. Villasana, "Epidemic Cholera in Texas, 1833–1834," *Southwestern Historical Quarterly* 40, no. 3 (1937): 216–30.

17. Emmanuel Domenech, *Missionary Adventures in Texas and Mexico: A Personal Narrative of Six Years' Sojourn in Those Regions. By the Abbé Domenech* (London: Longman, Brown, Green, Longmans, and Roberts, 1858).

18. It's estimated that there were six hundred cholera deaths out of a population of five thousand. Margaret Patrice Slattery, *Promises to Keep: A History of the Sisters of Charity of the Incarnate Word, San Antonio, Texas* (Houston: Sisters of Charity of the Incarnate Word, 1995).

19. Historical Marker Database, "Port Lavaca Cemetery," https://www.hmdb.org.

20. Federal Writers' Project, *Texas, A Guide to the Lone Star State* (Austin, TX: U.S. History Publishers, 1940).

21. Historical Marker Database, "Memorial Square," https://www.hmdb.org.

22. Federal Writers' Project, *Texas*.

23. Anthony S. Lyle, "Exhumation and Analysis of Two Historic Burials from the Camposanto at Santa Rosa Hospital, San Antonio, Texas," vol. 1999, article 2. San Antonio: Center for Archaeological Research, University of Texas at San Antonio, 1999.

24. Brevet Lieutenant Colonel J.J. Woodward, *Report on Epidemic Cholera in the Army of the United States in the Year 1866* (Washington, DC: Government Printing Office, 1867).

25. San Antonio Genealogical and Historical Society, "Bexar County Cemeteries," txsaghs.org/cpage.php?pt=35.

26. San Antonio Genealogical and Historical Society, "Bexar County (South) Cemeteries," Google Maps, https://www.google.com/maps.

27. *Index to the Senate Executive Documents for the Second Session of the Forty-First Congress of the United States of America, 1869–'70* (Washington, DC: Government Printing Office, 1870).

28. Lieutenant Colonel John Biddle Porter, *The Military Laws of the United States* (Washington, DC: Government Printing Office, 1911).

29. "Memorials Recalled as Names of Pioneer Dead on Old Cemetery Are Published: Funds Sought to Improve Burial Grounds of Early Dead of Community," *Fredericksburg Standard*, April 18, 1945.

30. "Plans Proceeding to Honor Pioneer Dead by City Cemetery Beautification," *Fredericksburg (TX) Standard*, March 28, 1945.

31. "Bicentennial Minutes of Gillespie County," *Fredericksburg Standard*, October 13, 1976.

32. "Cemetery Wall Re-Build Project Planned at Der Stadt Friedhof," *Fredericksburg (TX) Standard-Radio Post*, September 28, 2011.

33. Myra Lee Adams Goff, "The Year 1846 Was a Dark Year for the German Immigrants," Sophienburg Museum and Archives, July 10, 2016, sophienburg.com.

34. Greg Bowen, "Cemetery Plan Calls for Marking Mass Grave," *Herald-Zeitung* (New Braunfels, TX), November 26, 2010.

35. Hermann Seele, *The Cypress and Other Writings of a German Pioneer in Texas* (Austin: University of Texas Press, 1979); "Field of Graves Memorial: New Braunfels Cemetery Project Information, Concept Design, and Costs," New Braunfels Parks & Recreation Department, 2020, https://www.nbtexas.org.

## 3. Influenza

36. "Influenza Toll in Valley High: County Receives Load of Coffins; Street Cars Will Observe Rules," *El Paso Herald*, November 2, 1918.

37. City of Waco, Texas, "Greenwood Cemetery," www.waco-texas.com.

38. Hannah Hall, "Storied Central Texas Cemetery Undergoes $435,000 Renovation," 10 KWTX, September 15, 2020, www.kwtx.com.

39. David Segal, "Why Are There Almost No Memorials to the Flu of 1918?," *New York Times*, May 14, 2020.

40. Alfred W. Crosby, *America's Forgotten Pandemic: The Influenza of 1918* (Cambridge: Cambridge University Press, 2003).

## 4. Tornadoes

41. NOAA's National Weather Service, "A List of the Top 10 Worst Tornadoes in Texas History," https://www.weather.gov.

42. Bartee Haile, "Record Twister Strikes Goliad," *Hays Free Press | News-Dispatch* (Kyle, TX), May 12, 2021, https://haysfreepress.com.

43. Historical Marker Database, "Goliad Tornado of 1902," https://www.hmdb.org.

44. "Death: Wind Destroys City of Goliad, Tex," *Courier-Journal* (Louisville, KY), May 19, 1902.

45. "Ten More Are Dead," *Houston Post*, May 21, 1902.

46. Angus M. Gunn, *Encyclopedia of Disasters: Environmental Catastrophes and Human Tragedies* (Santa Barbara, CA: ABC-CLIO, 2007).

47. "Lott Cemetery in Goliad, Texas." Find a Grave, https://www.findagrave.com.

48. Raymond Starr, *Goliad* (Charleston, SC: Arcadia Publishing, 2009).

49. *Bulletin of the American Meteorological Society*, "Tornadoes," August 1, 1927, 125–29, https://doi.org.

50. Thomas P. Grazulis, *Significant Tornadoes 1880–1989, Volume II: A Chronology of Events* (St. Johnsbury, VT: Environmental Films, 1990).

51. Ibid.

52. Mike Cox, *Texas Disasters: True Stories of Tragedy and Survival* (Guilford, CT: Globe Pequot, 2015).

53. "Texas Town Wiped Out by Twister; Buildings Burned," *Salt Lake Telegram*, April 13, 1927.

54. John MacCormack, "Rocksprings to Remember Killer Tornado of 1927," *San Antonio Express-News*, April 10, 2017.

55. "Twenty of 170 Wounded Are Expected to Die; Bad Roads Hamper Efforts of Relief," *Vernon (TX) Weekly Record*, April 14, 1927.

56. Cox, *Texas Disasters*.

57. "Twenty of 170 Wounded," *Vernon Weekly Record*.

58. Historical Marker Database, "Rocksprings Cemetery," https://www.hmdb.org.

59. Weird U.S., "Lying Down on Smiley's Grave—Dallas," http://www.weirdus.com.

60. Other urban legends inspired by the grave include that all of the family died of a disease or in an arson attack that burned down their house.

61. One Dusty Track (blog), "Smiley, A Texas Ghost," https://1dustytrack.blogspot.com.

62. Tui Snider, Author and Speaker, "Urban Legends vs Cemetery History: Smiley's Grave in Garland, Texas," https://tuisnider.com.

## 5. Hurricanes

63. Paul Lester, *The Great Galveston Disaster* (Boston: International Publishing Company, 1900).

64. Ibid.

65. Ibid.

66. Ibid.

67. Ibid.

68. Ibid.

69. Ibid.

70. Ibid.

71. Ibid.

72. Galveston & Texas History Center, "Oral History Interview of Hyman Block," July 12, 2019, www.galvestonhistorycenter.org.

73. Ibid.

74. Galveston & Texas History Center, "Oral History Interview of Henry J. Bettencourt and Margaret Rowan Bettencourt," July 12, 2019, www.galvestonhistorycenter.org.

75. Lester, *Great Galveston Disaster*.

76. Ibid.

77. Ibid.

78. Galveston & Texas History Center, "Oral History Interview of Henry J. Bettencourt and Margaret Rowan Bettencourt."

79. Lester, *Great Galveston Disaster*.

80. Casey Edward Greene and Shelly Henley Kelly, eds., *Through a Night of Horrors: Voices from the 1900 Galveston Storm* (College Station: Texas A&M University Press, 2002).

81. Lester, *Great Galveston Disaster*.

82. Galveston & Texas History Center, "Oral History Interview of Hyman Block."

83. Lester, *Great Galveston Disaster*.

84. Ibid.

85. Ibid.

86. Ibid.

87. Ibid.

88. Ibid.

89. "Bodies of 29 Victims Buried in One Grave," *El Paso Times*, September 17, 1919.

90. National Weather Service. "The Hurricane of 1919," www.weather.gov/crp/hurricane1919.

91. "Corpus Christie Death Toll Now Figures at 386," *San Angelo Evening Standard*, September 21, 1919.

92. Texas Historical Site Atlas, "Site of White Point Mass Graves of 1919 Hurricane Victims," atlas.thc.state.tx.us/Details/5409012186.

93. Historical Marker Database, "Site of Indian Point Mass Grave of 1919 Hurricane Victims," https://www.hmdb.org.

94. Ralph Blumenthal, "At Last, After 85 Years, Baby Snookems Has a Stone," *New York Times*, November 7, 2004.

## 6. Fort St. Louis, 1688

95. Spencer Tucker, *The Encyclopedia of North American Colonial Conflicts to 1775: L–Z* (Santa Barbara, CA: ABC-CLIO, 2008).

96. Texas beyond History, "Fort St. Louis: Life…and Death in the French Settlement," https://www.texasbeyondhistory.net.

97. Ibid.

98. The most famous captive was Cynthia Ann Parker, aged about nine at the time, who assimilated with the tribe and gave birth to three children while with them. After she was "rescued" in 1860, Parker fell into a depression and died young. Her son Quanah would be the last leader of the Comanches to style himself as a "chief."

99. Historic Marker Database, "James Goucher," https://www.hmdb.org.

100. City of Bastrop, Historic Landmark Commission Meeting, "Agenda—October 16, 2019, at 6:00 P.M.," https://www.cityofbastrop.org.

101. Texas Historic Sites Atlas, "Details for Battle Creek Burial Ground (Atlas Number 5349008271)," https://atlas.thc.state.tx.us/Details/5349008271.

102. Texas Ranger Hall of Fame and Museum, "Surveyors Fight," September 18, 2019, www.texasranger.org.

103. Historynet, "Battle Creek, Texas—Where Surveyors Fought like Soldiers," https://www.historynet.com; Malcolm D. McLean, *Papers Concerning Robertson's Colony in Texas: August 10, 1837 through November, 1838* (Arlington: Texas Christian University Press, 1974).

104. *The United Service* (New York: L.R. Hamersley & Company, 1885).

105. Harriet Smither, ed., *Journals of the Fourth Congress of the Republic of Texas, 1829–1840, Vol. 3* (Austin: Texas Library and Historical Commission State Library, 1930).

106. John Wesley Wilbarger, *Indian Depredations in Texas* (Austin, TX: Hutchings Printing House, 1889).

107. "Last Survivor of Indian Massacre in Texas Dies," *Victoria (TX) Advocate*, December 11, 1927.

108. The next year, Dolly and Virginia Webster escaped to San Antonio; Buster was ransomed six days later.

109. John Holland Jenkins, *Recollections of Early Texas: Memoirs of John Holland Jenkins* (Austin: University of Texas Press, 1987).

110. J.H. Griffith, *Early History of Texas. Early History of Williamson County. The Webster Massacre. Williamson County Court House Sketches. Sketches of Early Days in Taylor* (Taylor, TX: City National Bank, 1920).

111. Texas State Historical Association, *Southwestern Historical Quarterly* 30 (July 1926–April, 1927).

112. Historical Marker Database, "Ripley Massacre," https://www.hmdb.org.

113. Historical Marker Database, "Proffitt Cemetery," https://www.hmdb.org.

114. Edith A. Gary, comp., *Recollections of Boerne and Kendall County* (N.p.: self-published, 1949), https://texashistory.unt.edu/ark:/67531/metapth836069/m1/208/.

115. Muriel Jackson, et al., *Families of Early Kingsland, Texas and Nearby Communities in Llano and Burnet Counties* (Kingsland, TX: Kingsland Genealogical Society, 1998).

116. "Whitlock Massacre Retold," *J. Marvin Hunter's Frontier Times Magazine* 14, no. 4 (January 1937).

117. Henry Smythe, *Historical Sketch of Parker County and Weatherford, Texas* (St. Louis, MO: L.C. Lavat, 1877).

118. Joseph Carroll McConnell, *The West Texas Frontier* (Jacksboro, TX: Gazette Print, 1933).

119. Colonel W.S. Nye, *Carbine & Lance, The Story of Old Fort Sill* (Norman: University of Oklahoma Press, 1937).

120. William T. Sherman to Ranald Mackenzie, May 28, 1871, Records of Edmund Jackson Davis, Texas Office of the Governor, Archives and Information Services Division, Texas State Library and Archives Commission, https://www.tsl.texas.gov/exhibits/indian/showdown/sherman-may1871-1.html.

121. Historical Marker Database, "Tenth Cavalry Creek," https://www.hmdb.org.

## 7. The Mexican War of Independence

122. "Descendants of Slain Soldiers Commemorate Battle," *Plainview (TX) Herald*, August 15, 2004.

123. Texas Historical Site Atlas, "Battle of Medina," https://atlas.thc.state.tx.us/Details/5013013310.

## 8. The Texas Revolution

124. Ron J. Jackson Jr., "Skeletons in Buckskin at the Alamo," *Wild West Magazine* (February 2021).

125. Ibid.

126. Joseph Baker and Thomas Borden, *Telegraph and Texas Register* (San Felipe de Austin [i.e., San Felipe], Tex.), Vol. 1, No. 21, Ed. 1, Thursday, March 24, 1836, https://texashistory.unt.edu/ark:/67531/metapth47891/m1/3/.

127. Thomas Borden and Francis Moore, *Telegraph and Texas Register* (Columbia, TX), vol. 2, no. 12, ed. 1, Tuesday, March 28, 1837, March 28, 1837, https://texashistory.unt.edu/ark:/67531/metapth47925/m1/2/.

128. Marilyn McAdams Sibley, "The Burial Place of the Alamo Heroes," *Southwestern Historical Quarterly* 70, no. 2 (1966): 272–80.

129. Bill Groneman, *Eyewitness to the Alamo* (Lanham, MD: Taylor Trade Publishing, 2001).

130. Scott Huddleston, "Mystery Surrounds Remains of Alamo Fallen," *San Antonio Express-News*, September 14, 2017.

131. Sibley, "Burial Place of the Alamo Heroes."

132. Jackson, "Skeletons in Buckskin at the Alamo."

133. Sibley, "Burial Place of the Alamo Heroes."

134. Groneman, *Eyewitness to the Alamo*.

135. Texas Escapes, "The Mass Grave of the Alamo Defenders," http://www.texasescapes.com.

136. T.R. Fehrenbach, *Lone Star: A History of Texas and the Texans* (N.p.: American Legacy Press, 1983).

137. Kathryn Stoner O'Connor, *Presidio La Bahía, 1721–1846* (Fort Worth, TX: Eakin Press, 2001).

138. Historical Marker Database, "Yucatan Soldiers' Burial Site," https://www.hmdb.org.

139. Historical Marker Database, "Amon B. King," https://www.hmdb.org.

140. Scott Huddleston, "Remembering the 'Goliad Massacre,'" *mySA*, March 24, 2011, www.mysanantonio.com.

141. Richard Bruce Winders, *Crisis in the Southwest: The United States, Mexico, and the Struggle Over Texas* (Lanham, MD: SR Books, 2002).

142. Sons of DeWitt Colony Texas, "Escape from Goliad—Isaac D. Hamilton's Reminiscences & Claims," http://www.sonsofdewittcolony.org/goliadhamilton.htm.

143. D.W.C. Baker, *A Texas Scrap-Book: Made Up of the History, Biography, and Miscellany of Texas and Its People* (New York: A.S. Barnes, 1875), https://texashistory.unt.edu/ark:/67531/metapth33001/m1/164, University of North Texas Libraries, The Portal to Texas History, Star of the Republic Museum.

144. Broadside 594, Address at Dedication of Goliad Monument, Broadsides and Printed Ephemera Collection. Archives and Information Services Division, Texas State Library and Archives Commission, https://tsl.access.preservica.com/uncategorized/IO_e8633427-0139-498a-817c-0d136105b223/.

145. Gary Clayton Anderson, *The Conquest of Texas: Ethnic Cleansing in the Promised Land, 1820–1875* (Norman: University of Oklahoma Press, 2019).

146. Lisa Waller Roger, *A Texas Sampler: Historical Recollections* (Lubbock: Texas Tech University Press, 1998).

147. *La Grange Journal*, November 15, 1928, http://www.fayettecountyhistory.org/monument_hill.htm.

148. The Historical Marker Database, "Monument Hill Tomb," https://www.hmdb.org.

## 9. The Mexican-American War

149. Karen Hastings, "The Forgotten War," *Texas Parks and Wildlife*, November 2007.

150. Thomas Bangs Thorpe, *Our Army on the Rio Grande…* (Philadelphia: Carey and Hart, 1846).

151. Eric A. Ratliff, "Human Skeletal Remains from the Battle of Resaca de la Palma," in *A Thunder of Cannon: Archeology of the Mexican-American War Battlefield of Palo Alto* (Santa Fe, NM: National Park Service, Divisions of Anthropology and History, Southwest Regional Office, 1994).

152. Ibid.

153. Thomas R. Hester, "The Discovery and Study of the Mexican War Mass Grave at Resaca de la Palma," *Bulletin of the Texas Archeological and Paleontological Society* 86 (2015).

## 10. The Civil War

154. Historical Marker Database, "Dead Man's Hole," https://www.hmdb.org.

155. James Alex Baggett, *The Scalawags: Southern Dissenters in the Civil War and Reconstruction* (Baton Rouge: LSU Press, 2004).

156. Robert Hamilton Williams, *With the Border Ruffians: Memories of the Far West, 1852–1868* (London: John Murray, 1907).

157. Frank Wilson Kiel, *Civil War Soldiers of Kendall County, Texas: A Biographical Dictionary* (Comfort, TX: Skyline Ranch Press, 2013).

158. R.H. Williams and John W. Sansom, *Massacre on the Nueces River; Story of a Civil War Tragedy* (Grand Prairie, TX: Frontier Times Publishing House, n.d.).

159. Historical Marker Database, "Treue Der Union Monument ('Loyalty to the Union')," https://www.hmdb.org.

160. "Civil War Atrocity Forgotten by Texas History," *Sioux City Journal*, July 28, 2013.

161. *J. Marvin Hunter's Frontier Times Magazine*, "A Bandera County Tragedy," August 1924.

162. Joseph Fish, "The Fish Manuscript, 1840–1926," Arizona State Library, Archives, and Public Records.

163. Matthew McDaniel, "Battle of Dove Creek Cost Many Lives 155 Years Ago," *San Angelo (TX) Standard-Times*, January 7, 2020.

## 11. Kentuckytown Hanging, 1864

164. *Weekly State Gazette* (Austin, TX) 15, no. 36, ed. 1, Wednesday, April 20, 1864, https://texashistory.unt.edu/ark:/67531/metapth181544/m1/2/.

165. Joe W. Chumbley, *Kentucky Town and Its Baptist Church: Or, Ann Eliza and Pleasant Hill* (Houston, TX: D. Armstrong Company, 1975).

166. "Century-Old Story of Massacre at CTX Jail Leaves Haunting Questions," *KXXV*, October 31, 2018, www.kxxv.com.

167. Denise Karimkhani, "Early Bell County Jail," Clio: Your Guide to History, December 16, 2021, https://theclio.com.

168. "Bodies of Four Hassel Victims Are Found Under House: Slayer of Nine Is Proven Murderer of Woman, Three Children," *Healdsburg (CA) Tribune*, February 2, 1927.

169. "Farmer Kills 9 in Family Tries Suicide," *Winslow (AZ) Daily Mail*, December 26, 1926.

170. Historical Marker Database, "Olivet Cemetery," https://www.hmdb.org.

171. "Cavalry to Quell Outbreak in Texas," *New York Times*, August 1, 1910.

172. Coshandra Dillard, "1910 East Texas Massacre at Slocum a Story That 'Needed to Be Told'," *Tyler (TX) Morning Telegraph*, October 21, 2014.

173. Tim Madigan, "Texas Marks Racial Slaughter More Than a Century Later," *Washington Post*, January 16, 2016.

174. Amy French, "Descendant of Massacre Answers Call of Her Ancestors," *Palestine (TX) Herald-Press*, July 28, 2021.

175. Coshandra Dillard, "'Slocum Massacre' Descendants to Converge at Site of Killings This Weekend for Historical Marker Dedication," *Tyler Morning Telegraph*, January 13, 2016.

176. Michael Barajas, "Where the Bodies Are Buried," *Texas Observer*, July 15, 2019.

177. "State Department Probes Execution of Mexican Peons," *El Paso Morning Times*, February 8, 1918.

178. "2000/168-Volume2 February 8 to February 11, 1919, Texas Joint Committee of the House and Senate in the Investigation of the Texas State Ranger Force transcript of proceedings," Archives and Information Services Division, Texas State Library and Archives Commission, https://tsl.access.preservica.com/uncategorized/IO_d93f2c79-dd04-4ad6-bf24-e136b62faf47/.

179. Ibid.

180. Sachi McClenden, "Amateur Historian Continues to Raise Awareness of Porvenir Massacre," *Big Ben (TX) Sentinel*, August 11, 2021.

## 12. The Truly Unknown

181. "University Team to Examine Skeletons." UPI, October 15, 1980, www.upi.com.

182. Find a Grave. "Chinese Common Grave Unknown," https://www.findagrave.com.

183. Historical Marker Database, "Emigrants' Crossing (20 mi. SE)," https://www.hmdb.org.

184. Patrick Dearen, *Crossing Rio Pecos* (Fort Worth: Texas Christian University Press, 1996).

185. Historical Marker Database, "Gonzales City Cemetery," https://www.hmdb.org.

186. Murray Montgomery, "Times Past," *Gonzales (TX) Inquirer*, October 17, 2004, https://gonzalesinquirer.com.

187. Murray Montgomery, "Mass Grave in Gonzales, Texas, 1905," Texas Escapes, October 2000, www.texasescapes.com.

188. "Nineteen Skeletons in a Grave," *Frontier Times Magazine* 4, no. 5 (February 1927).

189. Leslie Rangel, "University of Texas Researchers Fight to Preserve Mexican-American Burial Lands," FOX 7 Austin, April 2, 2021, www.fox7austin.com.

190. Marisa Charpentier, "'This Is Sacred Ground': Austinites and Researchers Seek to Restore Mexican-American Cemeteries in Montopolis," KUT 90.5, July 7, 2021, https://www.kut.org/austin.

## 13. The Disinterred or Disregarded

191. "Survivors, Residents Remember Sanderson Flood of 1965 50 Years Later," News West 9, July 2, 2015, https://www.newswest9.com.

192. Loretta Overton, "Our Reporter's Eye-View: Flood Battered Sanderson Tells of Heroism, Terror," *El Paso Herald-Post*, June 14, 1965.

193. Find a Grave. "Cedar Grove Cemetery," https://www.findagrave.com.

194. National Park Service, "San Antonio National Cemetery, San Antonio, Texas," https://www.nps.gov.

195. While ten Black soldiers were awarded the Medal of Honor for the same battle, as the list was alphabetical, Private Barnes is considered the first. Michael Lee Lanning, *The Veterans Cemeteries of Texas* (College Station: Texas A&M University Press, 2018).

196. Three other Medal of Honor winners are also buried in the same mass grave of the unknowns.

197. Bryant, ed., *Handbook of Death & Dying*.

198. John Watson, "The County Farm—Otherwise Known as the Poor Farm," *Cleburne (TX) Times-Review*, January 4, 2010.

199. Todd Glasscock, "In the Poor House," *Cleburne Times-Review*, February 7, 2017.

200. Carol Fowler, "A Disgrace…" *Austin American-Statesman*, July 2, 1967.

201. Kiah Collier, "County Pauper Cemetery Used to Be Full of Life," *Houston Chronicle*, July 11, 2014.

202. "Will Remove Bodies from County Farm," *San Antonio Light*, July 27, 1913.

203. Historical Marker Database, "Phillips Memorial Cemetery: A Historic Texas Cemetery," https://www.hmdb.org.

204. Hester A. Davis, "Public Archaeology Forum," *Journal of Field Archaeology* 22, no. 3 (1995): 349–53.

205. Jessie Degollado, "Lost African-American Cemeteries Located in SA," KSAT, February 17, 2017, www.ksat.com.

206. Paula Allen, "Removal of Remains in Old African American Cemetery Shrouded in Mystery," *San Antonio Express-News*, February 17, 2018.
207. Ibid.
208. Vincent Davis, "Historian Leads Project to Reclaim Acreage of Rediscovered San Antonio African American Cemetery," *San Antonio Express-News*, February 7, 2021.

## 14. Industrial Accidents and the Toll of Neglect

209. Mel Brown, *Chinese Heart of Texas: The San Antonio Community (1875–1975)* (N.p.: Lily on the Water Publishers, 2005).
210. Bob Bowman, "East Texas Sawmill Town Rose from the Ashes," *Houston Chronicle*, June 3, 2012.
211. "Rotarians Hear State Chemist," *Marshall (TX) News Messenger*, September 25, 1947.
212. Robert Arnold, "Remembering the Victims of Houston's Deadliest Fire," KPRC, August 28, 2018, www.click2houston.com.
213. Ibid.
214. J.R. Gonzales, "70 Years Ago: The Deadliest Disaster in Houston's History," *Houston Chronicle*, September 7, 2013.
215. Monica Rhor, "Discovery of African-American Graves in Texas Highlights 'Moment of Reckoning,'" *USA Today*, December 28, 2018.
216. Ibid.
217. Douglas A. Blackmon, *Slavery by Another Name: The Re-Enslavement of Black Americans from the Civil War to World War Two* (London: Icon Books, 2012).
218. Meagan Flynn and Lindsey Bever, "A Mass Grave—and Chilling Secrets from the Jim Crow Era—May Halt Construction of a School in Texas," *Washington Post*, November 19, 2018.
219. Rhor, "Discovery of African-American Graves in Texas."
220. John Carlos Frey, "Graves of Shame," *Texas Observer*, April 20, 2019.
221. Ibid.
222. Ibid.
223. "7-3 Homeland Security QA—Final," Speech files, Texas Governor Rick Perry Press Office records, Archives and Information Services Division, Texas State Library and Archives Commission, https://tsl.access.preservica.com/uncategorized/IO_291b7e23-99c7-4cfc-b21b-4f3356ca32ab/.
224. "6-23 McAllen," Speech files, Texas Governor Rick Perry Press Office records, Archives and Information Services Division, Texas State Library and Archives Commission, https://tsl.access.preservica.com/uncategorized/IO_735e49d9-23a6-4221-b342-382b674937d2/.
225. Frey, "Graves of Shame."

226. Joey Gomez, "Canales: We Don't Do Mass Graves in USA," *Rio Grande Guardian* (McAllen, TX), September 29, 2015.

227. Lomi Kriel, "Volunteers Seeking to ID Bodies Found Near Border," *Houston Chronicle*, July 3, 2015.

## *Author's Note*

228. Kenneth E. Foote, *Shadowed Ground: America's Landscapes of Violence and Tragedy* (Austin: University of Texas Press, 2013).

229. Dillard, "1910 East Texas Massacre at Slocum," *Tyler Morning Telegraph*.

# ABOUT THE AUTHOR

Kathy Benjamin is a writer, editor and humorist whose work has appeared on sites including MentalFloss.com, Cracked.com and Grunge.com. She is the author of *Funerals to Die For: The Craziest, Creepiest, and Most Bizarre Funeral Traditions and Practices Ever* (Adams Media, 2013) and *It's Your Funeral! Plan the Celebration of a Lifetime—Before It's Too Late* (Quirk, 2021). She lives in Austin, Texas, with her husband, Simon, and dog, Briscoe.